Advance praise for *Teaching Innovation and Entrepreneurship*

'Economic growth is now the world's top priority, and the only way to generate growth is through greater numbers of innovative entrepreneurs. Yet the question of how to foster them remains much disputed. Can innovation be taught? Can entrepreneurs be trained? With remarkable scope and depth, Charles Hampden-Turner not only answers these questions but also produces a work of great insight. This book should serve as the manual for twenty-first century economic growth.'

CARL SCHRAM, Ewing M. Kauffman Foundation

'If the global business landscape is more and more shaped by innovation and entrepreneurship, then, by demonstrating how it may be taught, Professor Charles Hampden-Turner is at the leading edge of world business thinking. Breaking through the boundaries of the conventional classroom, the Singapore experiment is about how to teach international students in an international setting. Yet, perhaps above all, drawing on his admirably comprehensive knowledge spanning a wide spectrum of fields, the author shows why business teachers have to search for "not things in some limited space but a pervasive pattern of connectivity" so as to create their own innovative, effective teaching solutions. An entertaining read that combines academic rigour with practical wisdom, this is a rare as well as timely book for the world of business education.'

WEI WANG, Managing Director of 2W China Investment Consulting Ltd and author of *The China Executive* (2006)

'Since entrepreneurship and innovation have become the watchwords for so many commentators seeking to predict the qualities and characteristics needed by tomorrow's successful leaders, the questions "Can capabilities in these activities be taught?" and "If so, by what means?" seem to be amongst the most important such questions for academics, policy makers and business people to be able to answer. Charles Hampden-Turner, in his search for answers, has produced a work of telling rigour which makes compelling reading. "Entrepreneurship and Innovation CAN be taught!" he concludes, and sets out to prove the assertion in thorough academic form, describing a wonderful piece of research. Of course, such work throws up more questions and will lead to more excellent research – groundbreaking work always does that."

ALAN BARRELL, Professor and Entrepreneur in Residence, Centre for Entrepreneurial Learning, Judge Business School, University of Cambridge

'Hampden-Turner is a prophet of innovative pedagogy. With great good fortune he and the Technopreneurship and Innovation Program (TIP) at NTU discovered one another.'

ANTHONY TEO, Secretary to Nanyang Technological University (NTU), Singapore

'What an inspiring and innovative book! The book provides a review of breakthrough in education innovations.'

MICHAEL SONG, Charles N. Kimball MRI/Missouri Endowed Chair in Management of Technology and Innovation, Henry W. Bloch School of Business and Public Administration, University of Missouri-Kansas City

Teaching Innovation and Entrepreneurship

Is it possible to teach someone to be an entrepreneur? Is innovation something that can be assessed and taught in a classroom?

Teaching Innovation and Entrepreneurship answers these and other questions by focusing on a teaching experiment in Singapore at Nanyang Technological University, wherein classes of English-speaking Singaporeans and Mandarin-speaking students from the People's Republic of China were subjected to an 'entrepreneurial eco-system'. Extending from the west coast of the USA to Singapore and Shanghai, this programme subjects students to a wide range of activities, including a four-month business simulation game where teams of students select their favourite inventions and pitch them to real venture capitalists with the inventors present. Drawing on the lessons learned from this highly successful experiment, the book argues that not only is it possible to describe the innovative process, we can also teach it, measure it, evaluate it and model it.

CHARLES HAMPDEN-TURNER is currently a consulting supervisor at the Institute for Manufacturing at the Engineering School at Cambridge University. He was Hutchinson Visiting Scholar to China in 2002 and Goh Tjoe Kok Distinguished Visiting Professor to Nanyang Technological University in Singapore in 2003. He did the narration and screenplay for a documentary film *Innovation and the Fate of Nations* in 2009. The third edition of a *Riding the Whirlwind* with his partner, Fons Trompenaars, was published in the same year. Their earlier book *Riding the Waves of Culture* (1997) has sold more than a quarter of a million copies in English and has been translated into nineteen languages.

Teaching Innovation and Entrepreneurship

Building on the Singapore Experiment

CHARLES HAMPDEN-TURNER

CAMBRIDGE UNIVERSITY PRESS
Cambridge, New York, Melbourne, Madrid, Cape Town, Singapore, São Paulo, Delhi

Cambridge University Press
The Edinburgh Building, Cambridge CB2 8RU, UK

Published in the United States of America by Cambridge University Press,
New York

www.cambridge.org
Information on this title: www.cambridge.org/9780521760706

First published 2009

Printed in the United Kingdom at the University Press, Cambridge

A catalogue record for this publication is available from the British Library

Library of Congress Cataloguing in Publication data
Hampden-Turner, Charles.
Teaching innovation and entrepreneurship : building on the Singapore
experiment / Charles M. Hampden-Turner.
    p.   cm.
Includes bibliographical references and index.
1. Entrepreneurship – Singapore – Study and teaching.   2. Technological
innovations – Singapore – Study and teaching.   I. Title.
HB615.H254   2009
338′.0407105957–dc22

                                                        2009011481

ISBN 978-0-521-76070-6 hardback

Contents

Grids

Dilemmas

Acknowledgements

I owe most to the man whom this book is all about, Professor Tan Teng-Kee and TIP (Technopreneurship and Innovation Programme) at the Nanyang Technopreneurship Centre of which he was the Director and founder. I was fortunate enough to participate in quite a minor way in his programme and witnessed his feat at first hand. Good teachers rarely gain more than a local reputation. In these pages I strive to give him the wider recognition he deserves. I am also indebted to the centre's new director Prof. Ray Abelin, who shot two films that featured this programme and with whom I discussed many issues raised here. Among particularly helpful members of the NTC was Prof. Vesa Kangaslahti who teaches technopreneurship to undergraduates with considerable success, also Ang Seng Yi without whose diligence I could not have sustained my efforts. My first inkling of what this course meant to students came from Denise Chng and without her I may not have taken up this cause.

Considerable assistance was received from Nanyang Technological University especially from its President Prof. Guaning Su and Secretary to the University Anthony Teo. I was greatly assisted by members of the Singapore government, most especially Teo Ming Kian, Permanent Secretary to the Minister of Finance, who conceived the word 'technopreneurship' in the first place and set up the funding programme.

In the process of shooting a documentary film about innovation I learned much from Professors Clayton Christiansen, Howard Stevenson and Theresa Amabile at the Harvard Business School and I thank them for their wise advice. While shooting at Cambridge University we conferred with Lord Eatwell, Master of Queens' College, and with Professor of Entrepreneurship Shai Vyakarnam, along with two famous entrepreneurs, Hermann Hauser and Gordon Edge. I learned much from all of them. The help and advice of Professor Alan Barrell, entrepreneur in residence at the Judge Business School, was quite invaluable, as was the friendship of Sir Paul Judge. I also owe thanks to Prof. Mike Gregory of the Institute for Manufacturing who provided an intellectual home for me. I am also grateful for the guidance of Wei Wang, author of *The China Executive* and managing director of 2W China Investment Consulting Ltd.

I practised the thesis of this book on two summer school classes at Sungkyunkwan University in Korea. For his kind hospitality and skill as a translator I am indebted to Vice President Kim, Jun Young and to Terry Henderson the coordinator of the summer programme that assembled students from thirty-five nations.

Professor Fons Trompenaars my business partner at Trompenaars-Hampden-Turner in Amsterdam was, as always, a rock of moral and financial support, as was Professor Peter Woolliams. Barbara Bloekpol is always there for me as is Theresa Hollema. I must also thank Professor Martin Gillo of Freiberg Technical University for his never-failing friendship and Salem Samhoud of &Samhoud who showed his confidence in me at a vital moment. Finally I am indebted to the staff at Cambridge University Press, especially my editor Paula Parish, who championed this work and never wavered. Without Clare Miller's feats of typing I would still be using two fingers and spelling words wrong. Without David Wong to troubleshoot my computer I might have cast it from the window. To all my students but for whom I would have lost my way many years ago this book is dedicated.

Introduction: a headlong assault on the inexpressible?

'Headlong assaults upon the inexpressible are not guaranteed to succeed', a wise mentor once warned me. Innovation and entrepreneurship are indeed indefinable. They cannot be defined in the sense of 'put limits to'. They break out, again and again. Innovation is a language and like languages in general can generate endless new combinations. In these pages I shall try to show how.

There are many reasons to be sceptical about the practicalities of teaching innovation. If such lessons are 'innovative' in themselves, then students who absorb this are being compliant, not original. Would not genuinely innovative students find fault with their lessons and rebel? Why would innovative teachers bother to instruct others, when by taking their own advice they could be enterprising, rich and famous? If we define innovation as making new combinations of existing knowledge, then is not the role of the university to impart that existing knowledge? How else are new combinations to be formed? An innovative physicist needs to know his physics. Teaching innovation to young people could be an invitation to cut corners and avoid accumulating facts.

There are also major difficulties about how innovative work is to be graded and assessed. How do you grade someone who has surprised, even confounded you? How is the merit of innovators to be gauged when the very definition of 'merit' has been changed by their contributions? Students who seek to enlighten their teachers might not get the recognition they deserve. It is a rare teacher who invites his authority to be undermined.

It is said that 90 per cent of all attempted innovations fail commercially. If the teacher applauds the innovative student the risk of serious commercial loss is high. If s/he warns the innovator, who none-the-less succeeds, then the teacher and the university become mere foils to brilliance. Clearly teaching innovation is a thankless task! You get the blame but not the riches.

Then, of course, there is the serious question of whether innovation is a rational form of discourse, befitting scholars. Innovative discoveries can be verified by rational means, by what the philosopher Abraham Kaplan called Reconstructed Logic,[1] but is actual discovery rational? Actual innovation abounds with accident and happenstance, the milkmaids that never got smallpox because cowpox made them immune, Archimedes happening to take a bath when vexed with the problem of estimating the volume of the king's crown.[2] This vital insight, occasioned when the water in his tub rose, belongs to the world of metaphor and analogy. His body became a metaphor for the crown. Two quite separate realms of being suddenly combined.

This is not reason as we know it. No less an authority than Professor William J. J. Gordon of Harvard University, the author of *Synectics*,[3] conceded that innovation was an irrational process, eliding mathematical calculation with bathroom ablutions and similar incongruous associations. We have to ask what kind of university would seek to promote irrational discourse, or want this in its midst?

It might seem that top universities do not even want to read of it. When James Dewey Watson offered his manuscript of *The Double Helix* to Harvard University Press,[4] the university president, Nathan Pusey, intervened to prevent publication. The book was too irreverent, describing some chaotic and quarrelsome scenes at Cambridge University during the discovery of the DNA molecule. He claimed the book was 'controversial'. It seems we are affronted by genuine innovation, even when it occurred more than a decade earlier on another continent. Innovation is too 'messy', too full of raw emotion.

Because innovation startles us, is unprecedented and unique, we begin to doubt that there is anything about it that can be generalized and passed on. Surely each case is *sui generis*, any lawfulness only emerging after the discovery is made? How can you teach that innovation has a recognizable structure, when suspending the existing structure and re-building this is what innovators do?

As for entrepreneurs, these are, to put it mildly, curious people. Historically they have been drawn from the marginal groups in society, the barely tolerated minorities. Hence Nonconformists, about 7 per cent of Britain's population, produced 50 per cent of its entrepreneurs in Ashton's *History of the Industrial Revolution*.[5] British Quakers contributed to industry forty times as much as their numbers would lead one to expect: Barclay, Lloyd, Cadbury, Fry and Rowntree were among the many Quakers.[6] A survey conducted in the year 2000 found that one-third of Silicon Valley's total wealth, some $58 billion, had been created by Indians and Chinese migrating to the USA after 1970.[7] In numerous cases immigrants have outperformed citizens in the countries they left, witness Europeans in America, and Jews, Chinese and Indians living abroad. French Huguenots were so famed for their enterprise that they were at one time forbidden to migrate from France. The numbers of top scholars, scions of noble families, fashionable insiders and products of our finest universities who become entrepreneurs are very few. For the most part entrepreneurs are a motley crew of diverse newcomers, obviously smart, but often strangers in a strange land, who surprise everyone, even themselves, with their success. They more nearly resemble the products of serendipity than of good order.

All this makes it problematic that entrepreneurship and innovation might be taught to people deliberately. How are we to simulate marginality and disorder? While it is true that entrepreneurs are typically immigrants, outsiders and minorities, these are also over-represented in prisons and in urban slums. Can we produce one without the other? The very challenges that entrepreneurs surmount to succeed may drive others into penury and despair.

There is a final telling argument. Were it possible to teach people to be innovative would not every nation and every culture strive to do this? There can hardly be an issue more urgent than creating innovative products. Standard products gravitate quickly to low-cost suppliers in China, India and elsewhere. Only ceaseless innovation can give high-wage, affluent economies the temporary monopolies that new products confer. If everyone wants innovation and there is no stampede towards educational breakthroughs, then it would seem that such feats have yet to be performed, or, if performed, they have yet to be validated. Validating such a performance is what this book is about.

The arguments against teaching innovation have all taken a similar form.

(a) If an instructor is innovative, then would not students simply comply?

(b) If instructors can do it themselves, why teach others?

(c) If innovation is a combination of disciplined subjects, should not the university be teaching the latter?

(d) If innovators re-define merit, how are they to be graded and assessed?

(e) If most innovations fail commercially, and they do, should universities be encouraging students to try?

(f) If the logic of verification is different from the logic of discovery, should universities teach the latter?

(g) If creativity is not a rational process, should universities dabble in irrational discourse?

(h) If innovation is controversial, might it not be better to impart to students what has been agreed?

(i) If entrepreneurs are typically migrants, minorities and outsiders, what becomes of the university's mission to civilize elite professionals?

(j) If entrepreneurship is characterized by disorder and disruption, how can this contribute to social order and good governance?

(k) Finally, if the ideal of innovation could only be realized, would not the rush to join this movement be in evidence? Where is it?

What all these objections have in common is the presence of two contrasting and often clashing values in seeming opposition. In short, these are dilemmas. This brings us directly to the definition of innovation and entrepreneurship to be used in this book.

It is a key characteristic of innovation that it resolves existing dilemmas facing people, and it is a characteristic of entrepreneurship that these resolutions are offered to customers for purchase. The combination of contrasting values is more precious and useful than their separation.

Let us consider the objections-cum-dilemmas one by one to see how these might be resolved.

(a) Innovation is not wholly within the instructors, nor within the students, but occurs in the *interaction* between the two, by leading out (*e-duco*) the potential within both.

(b) Teaching innovation is in itself a new project or service and is an enterprise in its own right. Teachers launch new ventures.

(c) Innovation is so potentially thrilling that denying students this experience is to deprive them of great potential fulfilments.

(d) There is no reason why students should not define their own goals and be graded on the standards which are self-chosen.

(e) 'Failure' is neither traumatic nor costly if it is merely simulated. Innovative education allows for many trials, many errors until learners get it right.

(f) The logic of verification is there to check up on the logic of discovery. The two must work together.

(g) Innovation is not rational in the sense of linear or technical reasoning. It is a form of encompassing or circular reasoning, as I shall show.

(h) Innovation is indeed full of controversy, but from this new disciplines emerge. The controversy is both exciting and temporary.

(i) It is part of the university's mission to extract from minorities, migrants, etc. the diverse abilities these possess, so as to qualify the current consensus.

(j) The disorder and disruption occasioned by entrepreneurship is the midwife of a new, more enlightened order in the process of emerging. Obviously those with a lesser stake in the status quo are more ready to change things.

(k) The ideal of innovative education is only now being realized. If we can establish this fact then the eagerness of many to benefit should follow.

Yet innovation is plagued by fakery and false starts. The history of 'progressive' education hardly inspires. The joust between traditional and progressive teaching is by now more than a century long and utterly sterile in its mutual opposition.[8] So long as each side of the dispute defines itself by opposition to the other side, nothing new can be generated. Breaking up this ideological spat and revealing its foolishness and barrenness is an important part of our work. Genuine innovation marries the old to new combinations, by joining discovery and verification, disorder with new order and making ideals real. It is this process of dilemma resolution that this book expounds.

1 Singapore's challenge

> No longer can we be just a production site for multinational corporations.
> We will have to be able to generate new knowledge and innovation of our
> own and commercialise them effectively.
>
> Teo Ming Kian, 'Empowering Technopreneurs'[1]

It is no coincidence that Singapore has been the first to take up this
challenge. It has world-class strengths but one major weakness, which
we shall examine presently. Colonized by the British, it had the good
fortune to be acquired by a benign founder. Sir Stamford Raffles was
very much a Renaissance Man, linguist, botanist and gentleman
scholar. Raffles is everywhere in Singapore, in streets, squares, quays,
drives, avenues, clubs and centres. He carved the whole city into
ethnic enclaves and built a free market. He was at heart multi-cultural
and defied the Foreign Office by announcing his annexation of
Singapore on behalf of the Crown before he had received permission
from his superiors.

Business Class on Singapore Airlines is called Raffles Class
and a Singapore Sling at the Long Bar in Raffles Hotel is a destination
for many tourists. I sought advice from the Permanent Secretary to
the Prime Minister's Office located in the Raffles Tower. Rarely
has a single name been put to so many uses. Singaporeans are comfortable with authority and have benefited historically from its good
judgement.

Singapore was cast out of the Malaysian Federation in 1965, which
had earlier gained its independence from Britain in 1957. Singapore was
not expected to survive, politically or economically. Its leader Lee Kuan
Yew, a lawyer with a Double First degree from Cambridge University,
was visibly distressed. How could one crowded city, without adequate
material resources, or even enough water, survive in any form? The
Japanese had overrun it in 48 hours in 1942. Its largely Chinese

population was suspected of Communist sympathies. The nation's prospects looked bleak.

And yet Singapore prospered. Its per capita income grew from US$600 in 1965 to $35,650 in 2007, ten times higher than China, with a purchasing power per head $5,000 more than Great Britain ($38,340 compared to $43,430).[2] It was more affluent than its ex-colonial master. But its achievement is much broader than this. For many years it has headed *The Economist*'s league table for sustainable economic development. Its urban landscape is immaculately groomed and beautifully maintained, proof, if this was needed, that a fast-growing economy can develop in ecological balance with its environment.

Among Singapore's competitive advantages, besides logistics and the world's biggest port for shipping, is that English is its working language among three others. This makes it extremely attractive to multinational corporations as an Asian HQ. In addition to this, its port facilities lie athwart the world's major trading routes, and are super-efficient logistically with a turn-around time which is the envy of rival facilities.

Because more companies wish to locate in Singapore than it could possibly accommodate, the government can strike bargains with those admitted which are highly beneficial to the state. Singapore's conviction is that wealth creation is learned and those who want office space and production facilities in this valuable location must carry out 'high end', knowledge-intensive work within the country, raising the skills of its work force, employing research graduates and thereby increasing the 'value-added per person' for the Singapore economy. There are incentives to join a 'cluster', a close-knit community of companies in the same industry supplying and buying from each other. There is now a financial cluster, a biomedical cluster (Biopolis), a water resources cluster, a digital media cluster (Fusionopolis) and an energy cluster among several others.[3] Those who wish to do simpler work, like adding water to syrup for Coke or Pepsi, are tactfully steered to Indonesia, Vietnam or Malaysia. Singapore actually penalizes companies for paying low wages by requiring a development levy on low-skilled work. Singapore's vision of world order is that nations find their appropriate rung on the knowledge ladder, buying what is simple from those below them and selling their own growing complexity to all comers.

One of the architects of the Knowledge Intensive policy is Teo Ming Kian, Permanent Secretary to the Ministry of Finance and head of the National Research Council.[4] He coined the word 'technopreneurship', meaning the fusion of entrepreneurship with high tech, or knowledge-intense innovation. It was he who in his days at the Economic Development Board of Singapore sponsored the Technopreneurship and Innovation Programme at Nanyang Technological University, which is the subject of this book.

Yet the Singapore government is very much more than a booster for economic development. Attracting as it does some of the top scholars in the nation into a Civil Service meritocracy it includes persons of considerable critical acumen. The emphasis on innovation came about, not because Singapore excelled in this respect, but because it was seriously lacking. In the GEM studies of entrepreneurial activity across the globe, Singapore ranked only nineteenth, behind other overseas Chinese communities. Something was obviously wrong and the plan to emphasize Technopreneurship was intended as a remedy. Teo Ming Kian put it well:

> In a way we are probably the victim of our own economic success. Singapore has had full employment for many years and our people led relatively comfortable lives in secure jobs. The rewards for venturing were not seen as commensurate with the risks of doing so. The environment was not supportive of such ventures.[5]

As the programme was about to be launched, Professor Tan Teng-Kee, its designer and founder, along with this author, wrote an article in the *Nanyang Business Review* which addressed the 'Six Dilemmas of Entrepreneurship' confronting Singapore at that time. The article is a clue to our thinking and helps explain the rationale on which the programme was based.[6]

We concluded that Singapore had long behaved and was still behaving like a 'Catch-up Economy'. These economies tend to take their cue from the values of already developed nations in North America and Europe and imitate their practices at lower cost, supplying the markets which pioneer economies had already created. This strategy is fine until the 'catch-up' economy actually draws level with its British and American rivals, at which point it needs to innovate and create markets, not just serve them. Singapore had reached parity. The time for 'technopreneurship' or innovation in high tech was now.

RIGHT FIRST TIME VS. ERROR AND CORRECTION

We argued that Singapore's education system was too oriented to 'right first time' application of technologies developed in the West. It ignored the contrasting logic of error and correction, by which innovative ideas are developed by trial and error and by successive approximations to an innovative ideal. So many Singaporean jobs owed their existence to technologies created elsewhere that the process engineers outnumbered the research engineers and the implementers outnumbered the originators. This was having a damaging effect on entrepreneurship.

In short, we located Singapore in the top-left corner of Grid 1.1. It concentrated on the application of knowledge already codified and

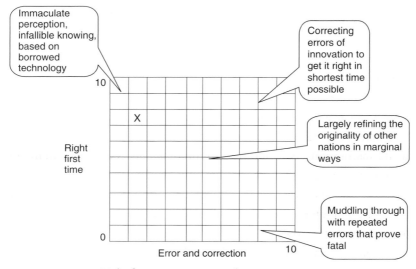

GRID 1.1 Right first time vs. error and correction

neglected the process of generating new knowledge by erring and correcting. The whole university system was skewed towards meeting the immediate needs of world-class corporations located in that state, who tended to overshadow local operators. The small and medium-sized companies from which most innovations come were relatively few in Singapore. We showed our grid to several experts and it was they who located Singapore on or about the letter X.

A nation cannot rely indefinitely on importing innovation from outside. Such products are insufficiently new and their life-spans tend to shrink. Moreover, the People's Republic of China has now adopted much of Singapore's catch-up strategy and has a huge domestic market to offer Western corporations, which Singapore lacks. It is for such reasons that the teaching of 'Technopreneurship' has become so urgent. The nation had to change tack.

ABSTRACT THOUGHT VS. CONCRETE OPERATIONS

We also detected a bias towards valuing abstract thought and devaluing concrete operations. This bias has deeper origins. The Chinese for many centuries admired the scholar and those who worked with their brains. China has the oldest civil service examinations in the world for those trusted with the affairs of the nation, who were stringently qualified to do so by learning classic texts. At one time it was the habit to grow fingernails long in order to demonstrate that you did no manual work.

Of course, the mastery of abstract concepts *does* save a lot of time. Centuries of research can be captured in one equation or formula. You cannot pass on what you know to the next generation without using abstractions. And yet the entrepreneur succeeds or fails in many concrete instances. The product either works on the ground, delivering what it promised, or it fails. The head and the hand must work together. The proof of success is found in concrete operations which deliver products and services contracted for you. You do not sell knowledge so much as knowledge embedded in tangible things. The concrete satisfaction is never far away.

One problem with those living and working near the top of the abstraction ladder is that they fear to step down. They are safe up there in the stratosphere where few comprehend them anyway. To come down to earth is to endanger your career. It is to expose yourself to the possibility that your intellectual thinking has no realism and no relevance.

Entrepreneurs have to go through the humbling process of putting real products into real markets and facing the consequences. This is more than many abstract thinkers want to face. It exchanges a guaranteed career as a symbolic analyst for the extreme uncertainty of betting on your hunch and failing with it. This is one reason why elites are rarely entrepreneurial. They do not care to put their status on the line. Entrepreneurship tends to derive from persons whose educations have been disrupted, like the Harvard drop-out Bill Gates and the dyslexic Richard Branson.

What seems to happen is that one's position on the status ladder gets elided with one's position on the abstraction ladder. Important people talk in generalities. Less important people run around and chase details. Grid 1.2 shows these contrasting values.

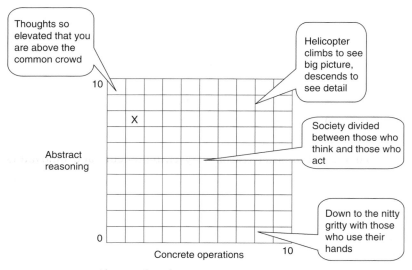

GRID 1.2 Abstract thought vs. concrete operations

The truth is that a product is only as good as the details all working as promised. What an entrepreneur needs is a Helicopter Capacity, the ability to see *both* the fine detail and big picture. Without the latter there can be no genuinely ambitious projects, but without the former the brilliant vision fails to work in practice. Unless people are willing to 'get their hands dirty' and spend all night in their garage or workshop to make it work, like Josiah Wedgwood, David Packard or Steven Jobs, vaulting ambitions are likely to fail.

EXCELLENCE PRE-DEFINED VS. EXCELLENCE RE-DEFINED

Singapore may be the most fairly refereed and uncorrupted meritocracy in the whole world, especially in commercial respects. It avoids issues of race, ethnicity, class and privilege by setting high standards and rewarding those who reach these. Bias is at a minimum. The level playing field is marked out and umpired. People are not equally endowed and those good at one skill may be poor at another. A meritocracy steers everyone towards what they do best by elaborate feedback on relative performance.

Unfortunately this seemingly splendid vision has flaws. Who gets to define excellence? Should young people single-mindedly pursue only those goals which their elders and the authorities deem to be worthy? Where is change to come from? One function of entrepreneurship and innovation is to re-define excellence. The innovator decides for him/herself what is valuable and strives to attain this. The excellence inherent in a new invention is unknown to the guardians of the status quo. You have to take this to the market to see if it is needed.

This is yet another reason why entrepreneurs and innovators are rarely top people. The latter symbolize older values and embody these in high positions. Such persons have gained the upper reaches of their institution by doing what was expected of them. In a very real sense scholastic and career success are self-fulfilling prophecies. You do well at kindergarten. Teachers and parents are impressed and from thereafter expectations smooth your way – unless, of course, you do something unexpected which could put your meteoric rise in jeopardy. In practice, those destined for the elite do not tinker with the escalator. One false step could dent everyone's acceptance of their inevitable rise.

If you accept the social and economic dispensation of your society then you would be wise *not* to try to re-define it. You are ascendant by the current criteria, so why change the criteria by which you are honoured? Entrepreneurship and innovation pose new questions, not just the questions and answers that were learned at school. Nature reveals herself to those who ask new questions, not to anyone else. A casual look around a Singaporean book store reveals literally hundreds of books on how to pass exams measuring intelligence and/or aptitude. These values are almost entirely American, but Singapore appears to bestow on these a universal validity. Singaporeans must measure up to, and preferably exceed, Americans in their own tests and criteria. What the genuine innovator asks is 'how can I demonstrate a process no one else has yet tried?' Rather than running in someone

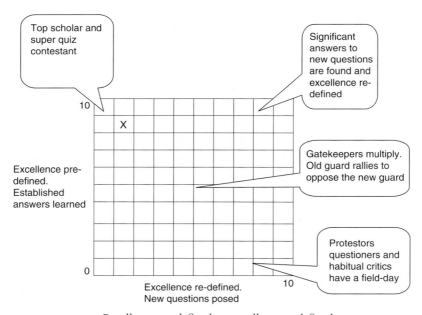

GRID 1.3 Excellence pre-defined vs. excellence re-defined

else's race, climbing someone else's ladder, you create your own. You start at the top and define virtue for yourself. Indians and Chinese in Silicon Valley are more likely to head their companies than to be manual workers within them. This is the quickest way to emancipation.[7] Grid 1.3 shows this.

Note that questions are just the starting point. You must avoid both the extreme of being a top scholar and super quiz contestant, who 'has the answers', and the extreme of being a fashionable critic for whom nothing current is good enough. Genuine technopreneurship occurs when you find significant answers to new questions, at the top right of the grid.

HARD SCIENCE VS. SOFT SKILLS

Chinese immigrants in many foreign countries have tended to put their faith in hard science and strict disciplines. One way to counter the prejudice facing a minority is to learn subjects where the answers are either right or wrong and the teacher has less discretion to mark you down. There is also the issue of students in the hard sciences being better disciplined generally and more willing to accept authority. The student rebellions in the 1960s and early 1970s in the US, Britain, France, Germany and elsewhere were largely concentrated in the humanities and social sciences, with business, engineering and hard science students noticeably fewer. There were disturbances and Nanyang University in the early '70's and although events were much disputed, it is beyond argument the university merged with the Nanyang Technology Institute and focused on training engineers, perhaps with MIT as a model. It evolved into Nanyang Technological University, established in 1991 without its arts and social sciences departments. In the last three years, Arts, Media and Design have returned.

While entrepreneurship depends heavily on developments in hard sciences, the ability to generate hope, mobilize enthusiasm, persuade investors and read customers all depends crucially on soft skills of personal and social judgement, which are usually associated with

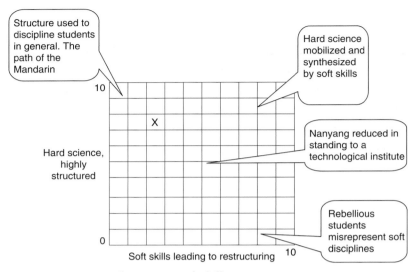

GRID 1.4 Hard science vs. soft skills

the liberal arts. With the vast majority of Singaporean male students studying engineering, business and the hard sciences, Singapore has neglected the arts of its own indigenous culture. It is not too sure where it stands culturally and might have trouble expressing this if it knew.

The dearth of culture stems from many years of ambivalence to China, its Communist forebear. If the Singaporean Chinese celebrated their Chinese roots then their allegiance to their English-speaking rulers might diminish. Chinese 'chauvinism' was officially discouraged. Much of the Singaporean elite had lost its mother tongue and too little has grown in this vacuum. If entrepreneurs are imaginative dreamers and idealists, what is there to dream about? Grid 1.4 puts Singapore once more in the top left-hand corner, pursuing the certainties of hard science and eschewing the uncertainties of turbulent, changing environments. What is needed for innovation to take root is much more emphasis on soft skills, on the imaginative arts, on stirring up enthusiasm and on encouraging those who see visions that are lost on other people.

EARLY DEVELOPERS VS. LATE DEVELOPERS

Not all brilliant people develop early on in their lives. Psychologists have distinguished 'early' from 'late' developers.[8] An early developer is typically a bright child from a good, close family eager for him to succeed. He/she works hard, without necessarily understanding why, because parental affection is thereby bestowed. High marks keep everyone happy, parents, teachers, authorities in general. As the early developer learns, it becomes clear to him or her why school work is useful and dependence on those who educate becomes even stronger. If such students are successful at university they may become Presidential or Armed Services scholars, and after education at a foreign university they return to Singapore to repay their bond, by several years' work in government employ.

This arrangement certainly produces very clever servants of the state, but whether it encourages innovation or entrepreneurship is another matter. Most innovators are late developers. They do not do badly at school but nor are they exemplary scholars. It is not so much that their powers develop 'late', but rather that the recognition of their powers takes longer. Almost from the beginning they play with ideas taught to them, giving more attention to what intrigues them than to the syllabus. This stops their grades from being the highest. They surprise their teachers rather than please them. Once in college they are more interested in the margins of their discipline, for example where it meets the world of enterprise, than in that discipline as a lifetime calling. They are also more interested in the places where discipline meets discipline because it is here that novel, inter-disciplinary breakthroughs are wrought. The 'lateness' of their development is also brought about by having to learn something about at least two disciplines before a new connection can be made. They need to think 'sideways' or laterally, not plough ahead like their specialist class-mates.

Inevitably such persons need to be far more independent, exploring for themselves rather than pleasing authorities, going to the margins of their fields, a practice often frowned upon, and making common

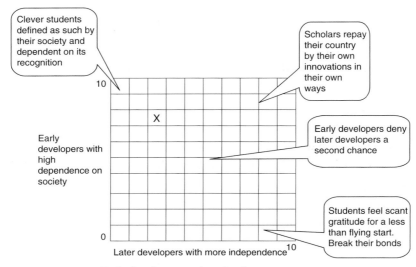

GRID 1.5 Early developers vs. late developers

cause with a rival discipline. The very fact that recognition of their abilities has been long postponed means that they are less dependent on others' approval, that they look further ahead and are prepared to take risks.

Singapore's habit of making top scholars repay their bonds may militate against innovation. Suppose an innovative student attends MIT and in his last year joins fellow students in an exciting venture. Rather than follow this star to fame and fortune, he must return to Singapore and repay his education in a role designated for him by his sponsors. By the time the bond is repaid, the venture with fellow students has succeeded or failed without him and he is years behind. When Teo Ming Kian asked to repay his bond by doing R&D he was told, 'you have your head in the clouds'.[9] Grid 1.5 shows the dilemma.

Again Singapore is at the top left. Its top scholars are too compliant and too distinguished to dare deviate. But the answer is not base ingratitude at bottom right, nor the kind of independence that scorns obligation. The answer is at top right, allowing scholars to repay Singapore in their own ways and through their own innovative contributions.

This concludes our view of why this Technopreneurship programme was urgently required, to re-orient Singaporean culture closer to the horizontal dimensions on our five charts and create a new synthesis between more dominant and more neglected values.

TAN TENG-KEE'S ATTEMPT TO RESTORE THE BALANCE

Tan Teng-Kee and colleagues set out to remedy these imbalances. To a large extent he was himself a counterweight to the excesses detailed earlier in this chapter. Ethnically Chinese and born in Malaysia, he and his wife are alumni of NTU, of which he is a passionate advocate since the university was founded by Chinese immigrant entrepreneurs. It is no coincidence that he has added a Mandarin-speaking course to his original TIP programme, attended by students from the PRC. He believes that 'the Chinese Century' has arrived and that after their triumph in the Olympic Games they will not look back. Chinese ethnicity is to be celebrated. It is time the majority of Singaporeans knew who they were. He is himself descended from educators. His great-uncle was the founder of Xiamen University. He begins and ends his programmes at the Chinese Heritage Centre, newly refurbished at the heart of the campus, to remind students who they have to thank for this opportunity and to what kind of cause the money they make should be dedicated. We must 'pass it on' so that every generation is better educated. Chinese civilization is founded on the twin pillars of education and the family.

Teng-Kee began his career not as a teacher or scholar but as an executive-cum-entrepreneur, selling two of his start-ups to China. He worked for Sunbeam and Electrolux in marketing new products and then received his MBA from Kellogg at Northwestern. Note the pattern of the 'late developer' outlined earlier, someone who had his concrete experiences first and thought about these at abstract levels only later, when completing a PhD at Cambridge University in 2002.

In effect, he has turned the usual sequence upside-down, acting first and gaining unforgettable experience and then reflecting on this subsequently with students. He is what Donald Schön called *The*

Reflective Practitioner,[10] someone in the thick of real events, who makes time to understand and promote the most promising of these. He was therefore in an excellent position to respond to five dilemmas which the two of us had identified. He corrected the errors of a life-time by teaching that innovation usually fails yet there are ways to stop this happening.

He reinforced the more useful abstractions which his students had already learned, but emphasized the concrete operations and myriad details needed to make these actionable and substantive. In this he appealed to all those who want to leave something physical in their wakes, who seek to change day-to-day realities. He taught that it was legitimate and necessary to dream, so as to re-define excellence with themselves as exemplars. Only those who know what they want and where their own strengths lie can realize themselves and fulfil their own ideals.

He deeply respected any prowess in hard science that participants brought to the programme, but he emphasized the soft skills of team-work, social engagement, colourful extroversion, playful persuasion and understanding others that were essential to restructuring a venture to make it new and appealing. He worked largely with late developers, not high-flyers in required formation, but those seeking more and casting around for something different. He looked for those who had changed their minds, switched careers, felt themselves to be in transition, were open to new directions and were vaguely discontent. He was in the business of offering second, third and fourth chances for genuine accomplishment.

We are now in a position to diagram even Technopreneurship, the central idea around which this programme was developed. Technopreneurship is the fusion of two concepts, high-tech knowledge intensity on the one hand and entrepreneurship and innovation on the other. We have placed these on vertical and horizontal axes respectively (see Grid 1.6).

It is a fallacy to believe that Singapore can 'win' the race to knowledge intensity, so long as it allows other nations to generate

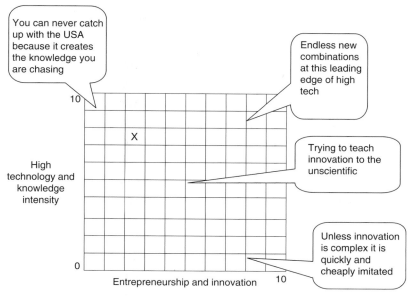

GRID 1.6 High tech reconciled with innovation

that new knowledge and simply tags along. Whoever invents and creates has a head start. This is the problem with Singapore's present position at top left. But innovative pedagogy that cannot stomach complexity (bottom right) will fail too, nor can you successfully teach innovation to the unscientific (middle). If Technopreneurship is to triumph it must make endless new combinations out of the latest developments at the leading edge of high technology – that was the mission of Tan Teng-Kee and of Teo Ming Kian his sponsor and it is this ideal which this book pursues.

2 The entrepreneurial ecosystem: a programme like no other

You do not teach technopreneurship within a confined space bounded by classroom walls. Of course, *some* instruction occurs there. It is convenient, but at least half the time is spent crossing real or metaphorical bridges to other realms. A famous psychological test of creativity is the Remote Associations Test.[1] The subject has to take two ideas, values or resources previously remote from one another and associate these in his/her mind. In other words, to create and to innovate you need to connect highly contrasting phenomena, so contrasting that no one connected them before.

If innovation comes about by combining a great diversity of resources then students must go in search of such diversity. But we are not speaking simply of crossing oceans and continents, although that may be necessary, but of finding when you get there a variety of cultures, political systems, life-styles and values. It is a serious mistake to regard diversity as 'a good thing', for reasons explained in Box 2.1. Diversity by itself has no reliable meaning. We need to see that with all values there is an implied contrast with an opposite value and a possibility to combine the two or to exclude either one.

Ecosystems are characterized by the richness of their variety, like a coral reef which makes a habitat for a thousand species of tropical fish, undersea flora and crustaceans, living among coral insects in an azure sea. The amazing colours encourage mate selection, so the beauty is self-sustaining and exists as one harmonious whole. It was the purpose of this programme to contrive an ecosystem rich in value differences and full of opportunities to combine contrasting ideas. Let loose among such colourful elements, the urge to innovate is spontaneous.

In this chapter I shall touch on a few of these contrasting qualities, yet making long lists of these is unnecessarily laborious, since one

---

Box 2.1   Is diversity 'a good thing'?

This is the wrong question for the simple reason that diversity is not a thing at all. Diversity like all values is a difference on a mental continuum within a person's mind. One of the problems in discussing values with other people is that we must often guess what mental contrasts they are making. We use words like diversity, courage and loyalty as if their meanings were obvious, but they are far from obvious. Diversity plays a very prominent role in human disasters like the Holocaust, ethnic cleansing, the lynching of Black Americans, race riots and the persecution of minorities in places like Kosovo, Rwanda, Georgia and Sudan. It is impossible to assess the moral value of diversity without discovering whether this particular diversity has been included. What is good for a culture is the inclusion of diversity; what is bad, even lethal, for a culture is the exclusion of diversity. Unless and until we know how the values of diversity and inclusion interact we are in no position to make a meaningful value judgement about virtue.

This rule applies to values in general. If the act of loyalty is to be a virtue the loyal person must be prepared to dissent. Nay more, the most valuable form of dissent is the kind motivated by loyalty. You dissent because you are loyal to your country and its leaders and you want them to reconsider their decisions. Churchill was being loyal to his country when he dissented against appeasing Hitler. Socrates was being loyal to Athens when he dissented against his persecutors. A fledgling democracy needs dissent. A person is truly courageous when this value is directed towards caution, when the warrior very much wants to go home again and enjoy a cautious life with those he loves. Similarly caution is a virtue when it keeps your powder dry, saves you for a more critical encounter in which courage can be displayed. If loyalty excludes dissent we rightly call it conformity. If dissent excludes loyalty we rightly call it subversion. If courage excludes caution we are right to condemn it as recklessness. If caution excludes courage we are right to deplore it as cowardice.

---

contrast begets another and it is connecting remote ideas in general that is important. We could mention past/future, thought/passion, play/seriousness and so on. Yet such distinctions multiply indefinitely and the trick is to combine these in novel patterns of enterprise.

One reason entrepreneurs act in unique ways is that they see different qualities and make new combinations among these. There are even important differences between the ecosystems of developed Western cultures like the USA and the UK and the 'catch-up economies' of East Asia who innovate in quite another style. Students in the TIP course are introduced to both. In the final section of this chapter I shall feature comparative ecosystems.

The programme starts in a most unorthodox fashion. Participants spend three to four days in an Outward Bound exercise managed by outside contractors in Singapore, similar to that used in training military commandos. They sleep rough, construct their own boats and shelters and perform challenging tasks in teams sharing the same adventures and confronting common crises. The purpose is to create team bonds among strong individualists. Fifty per cent of all subsequent course work will occur in teams, which, as Prof. Tan likes to say, 'are only as good as their weakest member', who could let the whole team down in a crunch, through an inability to provide a vital ingredient in a timely fashion.

This course dramatizes, as nothing else could, the fact that team members are actually and metaphorically roped together and required to place not just their minds but their bodies on the line, their heads and their hands. You are not only responsible for yourself but for others, because if any one slips then all could be brought down. They confront a series of unexpected challenges and must find a response. This may not be so different from entrepreneurship after all.

The programme now moves to Nanyang Technological University but not yet to the classroom. The next port of call is the Chinese Heritage Centre at the heart of the campus and a walking tour of the university's founding monuments. It is somehow appropriate to begin with the past and connect this to the future of the assembled members, for NTU was founded by immigrant entrepreneurs who made possible the very campus on which the participants gather. NTU was built on land donated by Ding Lin Sum with several other large contributions and many, many small ones. NTU was the first authentically

Chinese university, since the National University of Singapore was created after independence from a merger with the old colonial medical school. Some regard it, perhaps unfairly, as 'less authentically Chinese'.

Visiting the Chinese Heritage Centre is more than a symbolic exercise. Prof. Tan is a great believer in discovering meaning within ceremony. Those who founded this campus are an inspiration to entrepreneurs everywhere. 'They went from *zero* to *millions*', he explains. One of the major tensions an entrepreneur must confront is the almost limitless nature of success, compared to the grim probability of failure, yet those with nothing have everything to gain by risking themselves.

Prof. Tan also reminds them that even if they succeed they will go from millions back to zero again. Why is this? Because, when you die, you cannot take your money with you, which is why you must gain and give again, bestowing upon the community what you have gained from it and passing it on to the next generation. This is what he and his faculty are doing, passing it on to the next generation. When the class stands in the Chinese Heritage Centre they are surrounded by mementos of these feats, wretched refugees turned public benefactors. The purpose of the programme is to renew this received legacy, to find in the past inspiration for the future.

Only at this stage does the class enter into the Nanyang Technopreneurship Centre with its offices, classroom and break-out rooms for team-work. Indeed 'breaking-out' is a good description of the educational process. The walls are covered in press notices of new products unveiled by previous classes, of new start-ups launched, of tributes and endorsements this programme has received from the wider world. No member is much in doubt that this experience will be something different.

From their very first day in the classroom the participants are assigned to teams. Other exercises will place them in different teams, so that they engage with other class members, but for the moment each team constitutes an 'enterprise' and, for the entire length of the sixteen-week programme, the team will engage in a simulation of a real enterprise. They will make quick decisions and confront the results that flow from this. They will compare their intentions with what markets demand, enjoying success when not teetering on the verge of failure. This experience teaches them about fate-sharing, while they discover that each person, as a protagonist, can change that fate. They learn that there are no infallible strategies. All of these rely on feedback from the business environment, which visits them every week.

A word should be said about simulation, modelling and playing in general. The Simulation Game was created by Professor Michael Song of the University of Missouri. It is designed to be as realistic as a computer simulation can be. It represents a turbulent environment that has an order within its chaos and makes repeated challenges demanding a response. It represents something crucial to innovation, to learning and even to civilization. This is known as 'serious play', a capacity which in later chapters I shall measure.

There is no doubt that technopreneurship is typically serious. You can lose everything you have and if you borrow from relatives, as is common in Asian cultures, everything they have too! It would be hard to conceive of consequences more serious for the entrepreneur. And yet it is absolutely essential that your attitude is also playful and that you understand the connection between playing and getting serious.

Play is vital because it is the best way of making errors and correcting them. If you make an error while playing or simulating it costs you almost nothing and teaches you a lot. Much of the animal kingdom plays: think of lion and tiger cubs, otters, dolphins, puppies, kittens and monkeys. Nearly everything these young creatures must later do in order to survive can be learned by chasing, pouncing upon and wrestling with each other playfully, their lips hanging down over their teeth so as not to injure and their claws retracted within their paws. When such animals snarl and 'bare their fangs', then you know they are serious, intending the assault they learned in play.[2]

Play upon a stage is also a mark of civilization. Human beings can learn about tragedy without actually suffering, confront death without dying and ask 'to be or not to be' without having their fathers murdered. We learn about chronic failure by pretending to fail and by vividly imagining this. In short, imagining failure helps to avert it in reality. We survive to decide differently from how we did before.[3]

What characterizes innovation is long iterations from which uniqueness emerges. Thomas Edison famously said that he had not failed. He had merely found three thousand ways in which the light bulb would not work.[4] The Dyson vacuum cleaner is said to have gone through two thousand models and prototypes before its inventor was satisfied. The innovator must have the inspiration to do something new and the perspiration to see it to completion. Out of 'boring' repetition comes 'thrilling' novelty. The teaching of Technopreneurship must embrace both.

Yet this is not easy. When teams are encouraged to form theatrical troupes and give live performances, which act out their fantasies, those that are Singaporean hesitate. Children are raised to be modest, shy, unassuming and respectful of authority. The habit of showing off is not encouraged, and nor is the propensity to entertain fantastic possibilities. You should do more and talk less, so that your deeds exceed your promises. However wise this advice is, it tends to militate against innovation.

However, after a period of doubt, much briefer in the case of Chinese from the mainland, the students start to act out, dressing themselves up in fancy regalia and entertaining the class with skits and satires, all to general merriment and applause. Perhaps there is a potential exhibitionist in all of us trying to get out, which is rarely given an opportunity but once elicited gathers strength. It remains vital to make ideas nurtured by introverts be widely publicized by extroverts, and if the entrepreneur can switch between these roles so much the better. Before someone sinks millions into your discovery, you must learn to pitch before an audience and look confident, whatever your inner doubts. Play-acting is a crucial part of the process of gaining confidence.

But this use of fun and pretending is, of course, a series of rehearsals for the real event, by which time you had better be ready. You have a fateful rendezvous with your market, so now is the time to learn from your mistakes and put them right. Learn to laugh at yourself and you may avoid weeping later on. Better to fail in front of good, forgiving friends than among unforgiving strangers.

In a very real sense innovation is a succession of improving performances during which more and more allies are won over to your side, co-venturing employees, investors, loan officers, customers, JV partners etc. It is because you have something unfamiliar to impart that good communication is so vital. You need to make the familiar strange and the strange familiar, according to William J. J. Gordon.[5] Those you convert must join you enthusiastically in the push.

One of the most powerful elements of this programme is that students regard the course itself not simply as an entrepreneurial project, but as their project. It is an experiment which will succeed if they can make it succeed. It is not something done to them, but something they do. In the introduction we asked why those who teach innovation do not do instead, but in fact the programme is its own venture, which joins teaching with doing, learning with succeeding.

It is for this reason that members of the class become eager advocates of the programme. They invite speakers whom they know to address the class. They volunteer to interview next year's intake. They speak out at recruiting events, write cases for the class to discuss and write letters to the President and press. One team scored so highly in the business simulation game, better than any other team since the game had been invented years before, that they decided to apply to Professor Michael Song for the rights to distribute the game in much of South-East Asia, which they are doing now.

One consequence of fate-sharing, team-building and confronting challenges together is that the programme is not just a competitive arena like so many classrooms, but has a family atmosphere. Rather like veterans who went through a war together and never knew such camaraderie before or since, this programme creates close bonds between participants. Just as long as students compete to give the 'right answer' which is in the textbook or their instructor's head, so long will they compete for scarce resources with one person's prowess eclipsing another's. Everyone cannot be best, so that approximating to your teacher's own solution wins you high grades, while not seeing what is meant, or disagreeing, earns you lower grades.

But in this class there are as many 'right answers' as students have the wit to devise. The success of A, who is trying to introduce a heat-sensing device that will detect malignant tumours in the human body, and the success of B, who hopes to join craftsmen to collectors via the Internet, do not compete at all. Both can be brilliantly success-ful in different fields and not diminish the other. The family atmos-phere comes from transcending rivalries and from wanting fellow students to succeed. If they do, there is more reason to have confidence in the programme and what it taught you.

Of course, competition is not absent. Someone else may present better than you, enthuse others more than you, produce a better busi-ness plan and raise more money, but at least you can learn to emulate this and come up to the mark. Yet it is the diversity of aims that makes the unity within the classroom so palpable. We can all be 'best' at what we choose to do differently. 'What are we?' cries Tan Teng-Kee rhetori-cally. 'A family', shouts the class, and so they are.

That affection runs deep among those who face formidable and similar challenges was testified to by Denise Chng.

> In the middle of the TIP course my mother died. The class knew that
> I was worried about her but when it happened I slipped away without
> bothering anyone. It was my tragedy not theirs. Only one or two
> people knew where I lived. It was some distance away. Most of us are
> in debt and frantically busy with team-work, so I went back for the
> funeral alone. I was sitting in the front pew in the church and could
> hear the congregation assemble but not see it. When the congregation
> rose, I turned around. One third of the congregation were my class-
> mates. I was amazed and deeply touched that so many would come so
> far. We really *were* a family. I'm still in touch with most of them.[6]

Both the TIP programme and the University President Guaning Su received many letters of testament from students who took these classes. A sample is in Box 2.2.

Box 2.2 Tributes by TIP students

'The fire was lit by Prof. Tan and his exhortation to live your dream. I have never looked back. We are proud to be the sons and daughters of TIP.'

Frederick Wong, Moo Woo Design Pte Ltd

'Two years after graduating from this course I am embarking on a journey to make this dream a reality. We are people in search of excellence in whatever we do.'

Dr Saw Lin Kiat, Healthlife Pte Ltd

'I feel like I have learned and grown more in the last four months than in the three years of my undergraduate studies. TIP has nurtured me to be a stronger individual and has allowed me to explore and stretch my limits. It is not another class … it is a family.'

Ms Poh Keng Pei, Sales/HR Exec. Allglass Services

'TIP opened up my mind so that I could follow my passion … I never knew I could achieve so much. This confidence will see me through the darkest moment.'

Ms Chew Jianying, Exec. Great Eastern

'I have learned that there is so much more than having a good idea if you want to launch a business. TIP taught me to be patient and detailed. We have to stand up and be different. That is the entrepreneurial spirit.'

Ms Javiny Lim Yiing Wei, SM Motors

'Information was all isolated in my undergraduate days. It took TIP to bring it all together … the process was exhilarating … TIP blessed me with companions that were passionate. They were fighters, failed-but-won't-give-up. It was one of the most amazing programs I have ever attended and by far the best.'

Ms Ong Ai Ghee, Semb Corp. Logistics Ltd

Great eras of creativity in world history have occurred when protagonists knew each other. They did not always like each other but were passionately engaged in similar pursuits and deeply involved in their shared callings. And in the same community were sponsors, impresarios, critics and deeply appreciative audiences. It is the whole ecosystem that rises up and then in a few more years is gone, as each golden age passes.

It is important to this programme that its experimentation is eagerly watched over by sponsors, friends and visitors. That 50 per cent of the fees were, until 2007, paid for by the Singapore Government gave participants a sense of the importance of what they were doing. Every year on the NTU campus there is a Business Plan competition. Since nearly all the graduate schools now have at least one seminar in entrepreneurship competition is fierce. Yet TIP students have won every contest staged thus far. There is, in addition, an annual Innovation Fair at which would-be entrepreneurs take booths, display their ideas and engage visitors. It is proving a highly popular event and it adds to the general feeling that the ecosystems want their members to be innovative. Additionally, there is a steady stream of visitors peering into the classroom, attending presentations and generally contributing to the sense of occasion, as do the cameras of film-makers trying to capture the scene for posterity.

If the unifying of diversity can make a contribution to innovation, then the composition of the class and of the faculty are important. There are, or have been, students from the USA, the UK, Sweden, Hungary and France, as well as India, Malaysia, China, Indonesia and Thailand. Partly because of the scholarship system half or more are Singaporean although even these are of Chinese, Malaysian, Indian and Muslim backgrounds. The faculty are from China, Hong Kong, the USA, the UK, Finland and France in addition to Singaporeans.

THE LEARNING JOURNEY

After the first two months the programme begins a series of travels. The English-speaking programme goes to China and the USA. The Mandarin-speaking programme taught in Shanghai goes to Singapore and on to the USA. The two programmes meet in Shanghai, share experiences and projects and try to bridge the language gap via the few who speak both languages fluently.

Note the very wide contrasts between the two nations visited: the USA is developed and China is developing. The first is relatively affluent, the second still relatively poor. The USA is the world's champion of out-and-out capitalism, the PRC calls itself a 'socialist market-driven economy'. America extols laissez-faire even if the size of the defence budget belies this, while the PRC remains controlled by a one-party State. The USA is individualist, China largely communitarian. The first speaks much of human rights, the second of harmonious relations.

In all these crucial differences Singapore remains in the middle, influenced alike by both West and East, with a government which intervenes more than that of the USA but less than that of China. It is also in a very good position to knit these contrasts together in innovative combinations. For the growth of China is more than impressive, it is quite astounding. Not even Western in its outlook, its present growth rate will, if continuing to 2009, make it the fastest-growing economy in the history of the world, faster even than Japan in its heyday. The secret, whatever it is, has still to be discovered. In the meantime, the curious gather and the significance of being of Chinese descent assumes new meaning.

The programme moves on to the West Coast of the USA and now the students visit the most innovative regions on earth. The centre of US activities is the University of Washington in Seattle, not far from Prof. Tan's American home. It is here that science and commerce make a potentially fruitful meeting, not to mention biology and medicine, an industry the Singapore government has targeted.[7] Students, still in their teams, visit the bio-engineering department, attend presentations of the latest research discoveries and breakthroughs, adopt their favourites among these and try to turn them into commercial propositions.

This phase is crucial to the whole idea of technopreneurship. These are high-technology developments and understanding them and communicating this understanding to would-be investors is a major challenge. The climax of this phase of the journey is the visit by several real venture capitalists, before whom the teams of students must pitch for investment funds. The VCs give students detailed feedback on why they would or would not invest on the basis of their presentations. This part of the programme has proved very popular with the bio-engineers, who must often struggle to get their work recognized commercially.

While in Seattle the students work a shift in a Starbucks coffee shop to discover for themselves the internal design of a service system, which is nothing like as simple as it looks. Starbucks took a depressed business with slim margins selling supermarket coffee and turned it into a coffee experience with exotic beans from many different countries, non-exploitation of coffee growers and coffee-brewing smells wafted onto the pavement by extractor fans, together with an ambience that customers appreciated.

The programme moves on to Google, Microsoft, Boeing's new 'Dreamliner' and half a dozen successful start-ups, where the entrepreneurs and founders relate their stories and the products are demonstrated. The heady contrast here is between start-ups and mature yet innovative companies. Before they leave Seattle, there is a party at Prof. Tan's house on the lake, whereupon they move on to San Francisco, the Bay Area and Silicon Valley.

They once again visit a mix of start-ups and companies that have renewed themselves and maintained their innovative origins. Silicon Valley is famous for its immigrant entrepreneurs. As of the year 2000, one-third of these companies were headed by Chinese or Indian immigrants to the USA arriving after 1970. These are valuable role models for participants in the class and their case histories fascinate.[8] This area of the USA also offers an interesting lesson in the norms and values conducive to innovation, gender equality, gay toleration, equal opportunities, cosmopolitan life-styles, dense urbanization; precisely the values of an ecosystem of strongly contrasting elements in colourful propinquity.[9]

The class now returns to Singapore, or in the case of the Mandarin-speaking class, to Shanghai. It should not be thought that participants neglect new scientific developments right under their noses at NTU or Fudan or local venture capitalists, who are more likely than foreigners to provide investment funds in the future. The government has several special funds intended to assist entrepreneurs and these are minutely examined also.

By now the teams have devised their projects, not just pretend projects, but prototypes they seek to take beyond the programme into commercial reality. The Business Plan Competition is a chance to hone their skills, while the Innovation Fair at which they take booths is an opportunity to recruit fellow enthusiasts as employees, customers etc. A very important part of the ecosystem is the prototype/product distinction which has a natural affinity with the playfulness/seriousness contrast discussed earlier. You play with your prototype, which is relatively cheap compared with the expense of finished products. With prototypes you can make errors and correct these without suffering major loss. You can show the prototype to potential allies and heed their advice and criticism. There is an annual Innovation Fair at NTU where innovators dramatize what the product might do, to and for customers.

SUPPLY INNOVATION AND DEMAND INNOVATION

Even now the ecosystem development is not complete. A most important aspect of the programme is the contrast between supply innovation and demand innovation. Supply innovation is what people think of first, some life-changing products like the personal computer, a technological breakthrough. Relatively neglected, yet every bit as vital, is demand innovation. Are you able to make a new, useful combination within the customer's set of needs? This bridges the often yawning gap between *producer* and *customer*, a veritable gulf of incomprehension. However clever the product may be, the customer may be unable to use it, for a number of reasons not well understood. The real gain comes from addressing the customers' 'pain points', the difficulties they encounter in doing business. You move the customer from pain to pleasure.

For example, Cardinal Drugs once supplied pills in packaged lots to hospitals, a wretched low-margin business with many competitors. It decided to 'follow the pill' and see what became of it once it reached the hospital. Several 'pain points' for the hospital were immediately discovered. The pills went to the hospital pharmacy that was chronically under-staffed because of nation-wide shortages of trained graduates. The pills also went missing, leading not just to waste but to addicted patients and legal liability for the hospital.[10]

By offering to staff and manage hospital pharmacies, in addition to supplying them with drugs, Cardinal could make a profit margin six times higher than before. In addition, it supplied pill-dispensing machines in the nurses' stations, which disgorged pills only upon receipt of a recognized signature or thumbprint, and automatically billed patients. The pills no longer went missing. Another pain point had been assuaged and an additional margin earned. The distinction here is between *technology* and *anthropology*. Cardinal stayed with its core technology of pill-sorting, but it added an anthropological dimension that solved customers' problems.

CONVERGING INDUSTRIES

Prof. Tan also alerts the class to what happens when previously *separate* industries *converge* and cross-fertilize. Two converging industries are very likely to occasion something akin to the Big Bang, with considerable fall-out and re-alignment of resources. Examples include biology and medicine, electronics and mechanical engineering, computers and ever-shrinking disc-drives, photography and mobile phones, financial services and the Internet.

It is possible to observe these convergences and be ready for their collision or cross-fertilization. There are, for example, a huge number of ways in which electronics can monitor and improve machine functioning, or how biological understanding of the human genome can guide medicine. While specific innovations cannot be predicted, that numerous innovations will occur at the intersection of these disciplines is predictable and entrepreneurs steering in this direction will encounter many additional opportunities. This suggests yet another quality of an entrepreneurial ecosystem, scientific *disciplines* and *spaces between* disciplines. Alvin Toffler pointed out, as early as the 1970s, that the vast majority of innovations were inter-disciplinary.[11] It is there one must look for new combinations.

It is useful in this regard to distinguish *vertical* technologies from *horizontal* technologies. A vertical technology stands alone, like drilling for oil or gas, locomotive engineering and automobile production. Of greater interest to the entrepreneur are horizontal technologies, like the micro-chip, which many East Asian economies call 'the rice of industry' because it feeds so many other technologies. For example, a micro-chip opens your garage door and when placed in the horns of longhorn cattle they tell the rancher where the strayed cows can be located. There are literally billions of micro-chips in different products across the board.

Whereas thirty years ago only 10 per cent of the value of an automobile lay in its electronics, it is now close to 50 per cent. Safety systems like airbags, remote locking, automatically unlocked doors and location signals are all electronically triggered. If you follow a horizontal technology you can find thousands of new potential uses, as it crosses from industry to industry. Horizontal technologies include the Internet, liquid crystal displays, mobile phones and digital imaging.

This last technology is particularly useful to innovators generally, because it permits the visualization of an idea before it becomes a reality. In time, venture capitalists may insist that digital images of your project supplement, if not replace, the business plan. Such imagery is especially important when multi-million-dollar projects are being planned, like shopping malls or corporate headquarters. Those sponsoring such projects need to know what the finished design will look like, both inside and outside, and a virtual reality series of images may be essential to such expenditures.

PERFORMANCES AND PLATFORMS

Another useful distinction for an entrepreneurial ecosystem is between the stage or platform and the original performance mounted on that platform. Theatrical productions take place upon a stage and this is a fairly routine construction of wood, curtains, scenery, lights, music and sound systems, with backstage amenities. There are also elaborate resources like mirrors and make-up to supply what a production may need.

This gives us a useful metaphor for how innovation stands upon 'platforms'. A LEGO set is not, by itself, an astonishing product. Indeed, its yellow and red plastic bricks have been pretty standard for several decades now. What it more nearly resembles is a platform out of which a child can create over a hundred different buildings before a parental audience.[12] Such platforms are capable of further elaboration, so that in *Mindstorms*, mounted on LEGO's platform of plastic bricks, a child can create a robot, steered by software and an engine to propel the robot. Microsoft is similarly a platform, on which entrepreneurs can mount new applications. Mobile phones act as a platform for text messaging, photography and image transmission.

Over time a new product like the Internet may become a platform for thousands of other 'performances' mounted on top of it. Only a few miles away from Nanyang Technopreneurship Centre is an orchid farm, called Orchidville. Growing orchids was a barely profitable business, but innovations mounted on this platform were profitable. It began with orchid arrangements supplied to local hotels. Then similar arrangements were supplied to event planners, banqueting specialists and photographers visiting those hotels. After the success of this enterprise, the government was approached about having 'orchid-growing kits' in every primary school as a practical demonstration of biology, with the children caring for the plants.

The next move was into high-tech hydroponics, the growing of flowers in liquid solutions with many of the properties of soil. One huge advantage of this move was that test tubes of liquid could be affixed to the roots of exported plants so that they continue to grow in transit and last several times longer when purchased. Note that the core competence of growing hundreds of varieties of orchid remains the same, a crucial quality of this platform. The company now creates hybrid, customized orchids, named after the buyer herself. It provides scent made from particular orchids and has opened a tourist centre where visitors can drink, dine and dance among the waving flowers. A corporate hospitality facility is in the planning stage.

The notion of a platform on which new products 'perform' allows for a crucial distinction between sustaining and disruptive innovation. The distinction is made by visiting Professor Clayton Christiansen, who teaches on this course and is the author of *The Innovator's Dilemma*.[13] Sustaining innovation occurs on a solid platform. Disruptive innovation undermines the platform itself and creates a new one, in the way that ever-shrinking disc-drives undermined the computers built around this platform and mini steel mills undermined integrated steel mills.

COMPARATIVE ECOSYSTEMS, WEST AND EAST

Innovative ecosystems take more than one form and we must be careful not to assume that any one process is the best. In all events the trip from China to the USA made by TIP students exposes them to both kinds. Countries like the USA and the UK have prestigious centres of higher education like Harvard, Stanford and Cambridge. Knowledge-intensive products and systems often have their origins in the research conducted there. The start-ups surrounding such universities have commanded much attention. There is Rt. 128 around Harvard and MIT. Silicon Valley surrounds Stanford and there is a Cambridge Phenomenon around that university. These small companies are often able to make the connections between disciplines that the specialist structures of universities ignore.

Such businesses are often traceable to the 'pure' science of the university (e.g. the discovery of the DNA molecule), which then becomes a science applied to human uses (e.g. the Human Genome Project), which is then commercialized (e.g. new instruments and techniques for medical diagnostics). Developments spread outwards in wave-forms from their points of origin and may take several decades. What tends to slow this process, particularly in the UK, is the high prestige of 'pure' science and the lesser standing of even life-saving applications. Fortunately the days are gone when C. P. Snow could say in his Reid Lecture, 'We took pride in the fact that what we were researching would not be of the slightest use to anyone.' Even so you go 'up' to Cambridge and when you graduate you 'come down'. The USA is less prone to such snobbery.

Shailendra Vyakarnam, Professor of Entrepreneurship at the Judge Business School, Cambridge University, envisages an ecosystem around Cambridge University, which is linked up by skeins of knowledge joining earlier to later developments. His vision emphasizes the centrality of the university, together with Acorn Computers, the world's first personal computer, designed by an Austrian-born, Cambridge physicist Hermann Hauser. Although Acorn was branded by the BBC it lost out to Apple and the capacity of the huge US domestic market to set standards for everyone else. But the original team formed around the production of Acorn spread out into new surrounding businesses. Another catalyst was a major government grant for Computer Aided Design (CAD) equipment, which became the nucleus of a wide expansion. The metaphor here is of a multi-generational, extended family governed by mutual intimacies. Everyone knew everyone and their products shared common scientific themes. Later major companies moved in, Olivetti, GE, DAKO Diagnostics, Dialog, Cytomation, Western Multiplex, Microsoft, Philips and others.

Such ecosystems, of which Silicon Valley is the best-known example, move top-down, from abstract forms of knowing to concrete, commercial applications. These ecosystems are especially well suited to famous, science-based universities. But prestigious centres of learning like these are not created quickly or easily. Were nations in East Asia to wait on such developments, this could take decades, even centuries.

There is a very different innovative ecosystem in such places as Singapore, China, Korea and Taiwan. This kind moves in the opposite direction, not top-down but bottom-up, from humble, concrete accomplishments to more ambitious, abstract designs. It was given an initial momentum by the eagerness of Western-based multinationals to outsource their work to lower-cost regions. This has now occurred on a massive scale, but what happens next is instructive and for the West quite ominous, as is exemplified by the Singapore-based contractor-cum-designer, Flextronics.

Flextronics initially supplied circuit boards to the computer and printer industries. A typical customer was Hewlett Packard which had its Asian operations coordinated from Singapore. At this stage the sub-contracting was routine, a typical money-saving device, with cheap labour across the Malaysian border. Then Flextronics offered to supply the motherboards as well, a more challenging task but still common-place. One reason multinational companies readily agree to such arrangements is that they improve their positions in the eyes of the financial markets. A lower asset-base improves the profit-asset ratio, while lower costs increase profits. These are considered smart moves.

Flextronics next offered to assume responsibility for the manage-ment of the supply-chain and its logistics. Since its own components were now a major part of that supply-chain it was in a good position to maintain inventory levels and guarantee just-in-time delivery. Supply-chain management is not without its innovative opportunities. You essentially pull together resources from a global network of which you are the hub. Once again HP agreed. It was shortly after this move that Flextronics offered to design the brains within the original equipment itself, using the latest and most sophisticated integrated circuits from its new design centre in Singapore. It was doing this not just for HP alone but for several players in the industry so that it had become a crucial resource and a pioneer on the leading edge of inno-vation. This 'hollowing out' of the core competence of its customers had been approved at every step and places Flextronics in a virtually impregnable position as the brains of companies in competition with each other.

While Flextronics could become an original equipment supplier in its own right, competing with its current customers, it chooses not to do so. Its present position as the Intelligence Hub of the entire industry is probably more powerful. It supplies famous brands that need to maintain their reputations or perish. It is the power behind several thrones, the cooperative link between competitors. This stra-tegy has also been widely adopted by China, which uses both top-down and bottom-up approaches, depending on circumstances. The business incubator a few hundred yards from the gates of Fudan University in Shanghai has close to a thousand corporate tenants. The nearby university supplies both science and the rungs of the Knowledge Ladder for those who sub-contract to multinationals. In short, TIP students study both routes to high-level 'technopreneurship'.

SUMMARY

We have asked: what constitutes an innovative ecosystem? The answer is a designed environment with a number of highly contrasting elements, needing to be bridged and reconciled by the potential entrepreneur or innovator. The pairs of contrasting elements are italicized here. Such a person needs to *connect* phenomena which *contrast* and *combine* elements which are *diverse. Individualists* need to be bonded into *teams* by common challenges, using not just *heads* but *hands* and getting dirty. For sudden *challenges* they must find *responses.*

They are invited to value *past* entrepreneurs, so as to better engage the *future,* to *gain* millions and *give* it all away, to *receive* a legacy and to *renew* it. They are bidden to *play* but for a *serious* purpose, to *decide* and live with *results,* in a *simulation* of *real* business. They *share* a common fate, yet have *personal* responsibility for this. They devise serial *strategies* and face the *feedback.*

They must search out the hidden *order* within the *chaos,* by making repeated *errors* yet *correcting* these. By *imagining* failure, they avert its *actual occurrence.* From continual *iterations* there emerges something *unique,* as *inspiration* mingles with *perspiration.* Mostly *introverted,* Singaporeans are encouraged to be *extrovert* and show off, looking *confident* despite their *doubts.* They are *pretending* so as to convince themselves and be ready for the *real event.*

Each participant is in a *competitive arena,* yet they are sufficiently different and diverse in their aims that a *family atmosphere* also develops. On their journeys across the world they travel from a *developing* to a *developed* economy, from *poverty* to *riches,* from *socialism* to *capitalism,* from *individuality* to *community,* from human *rights* to human *relations.*

In the USA they try to make complex *science* more *commercial* and fuse *biology* with *medicine*, as *inventors* confront *investors*. They compare *start-ups* with *mature* organizations persisting with their innovation. In Silicon Valley they can see for themselves how immigrant *outsiders* from India and China become *insiders*.

Back in Singapore they use *prototypes* to stand in for improved *products* and compare *supply* innovation with *demand* innovation, thereby joining *producers* with *customers* and *technology* with '*anthropology*'. They learn to look at the *space between* disciplines, not just the *discipline* itself, and distinguish *vertical* from *horizontal* technologies. They learn that *original performances* may need a *standardized platform* as a resource base.

A 'platform' helps participants to distinguish between *incremental* and *disruptive* innovation. Incremental innovations use the platforms on which they stand to create a new product. Disruptive innovations disrupt the existing platforms and begin new theatres of operation. Finally ecosystems themselves can be *top-down* from *abstract* knowledge to *concrete* results, or *bottom-up* like Flextronics, moving from concrete operations to abstract designs. The ecosystem is the key to innovation.

3 How can innovative pedagogies be measured?

There is a popular phrase, 'it does not count!'. By this is meant that if we cannot somehow measure something then it pales into insignificance. Yet measuring innovation is a considerable challenge, made harder by the fact that being innovative or creative is very commonly faked. This fakery is quite rightly attacked and satirized. People can easily dress in Bohemian garb and behave in a bizarre fashion without being remotely innovative. While it is true that innovative persons have a large emotional stake in the outcome of their work, it is not true that getting emotional and flaunting an 'artistic temperament' is anything more than the affliction of amateurs.

As previously remarked innovative persons challenge the status quo, but the belief that giving a free rein to impulse will lead to some dawn of originality may be without basis. For example, student rebellions in the late sixties and early seventies did not go beyond protest and left few if any changes of substance in their wake. They even failed to persuade American governments not to embark on war against native insurgencies. But perhaps the most glaring attempt to counterfeit creativity was made by hippies and the counter-culture. They took every cliché of supposed artistry to an absurd extreme. They staged 'spontaneous' happenings in search of serendipity. They flaunted aimlessness, self-display and irresistible impulse.

In reality, this entire movement created next to nothing and left only beads and discarded incense sticks in its wake. But this phenomenon, brief as it was, should put us on our guard. Yes innovative persons are playful but so are doped-up revellers. Yes innovative persons are emotional but any child can throw a tantrum. There is indeed a measure of disorder in innovation, but simply being disorderly is no guarantee of originality. It is true that entrepreneurs are often outsiders, but simply being 'outside' does not make you an entrepreneur. It is true that innovators re-invent themselves but when the author lived in California the number of persons prattling on about the 'new me' told more of self-indulgence.

Every genuinely innovative person needs to be comprehensible. When Shakespeare writes in *Henry V*, 'O! for a muse of fire that would ascend the brightest heaven of invention', there is no word in that sentence unknown to a largely illiterate population. He has put old words into new combinations. This is what Arthur Koestler meant when he said that creativity gives you a 'shock of recognition'.[1] The shock comes from the novel combination. The recognition comes from the old words and their meanings. The whole is poetic. This is what William J.J. Gordon, a professor at Harvard, meant when he claimed that innovation 'makes the familiar strange and the strange familiar'.[2] The association between old parts and new wholes brings this about. Silicon chips are a lot more significant than the fine sand that goes into them.

Because we were anxious to smoke out any fraudulence or pseudo-innovation we asked ourselves, 'what *must* be true for innovation to be genuine? What would counterfeits *not* have?' We decided that genuine innovation required *ideas* that subsequently became *realities*: by this we did not mean mere objects, but products and services purchased by markets in which buyer satisfaction rendered the supplier profitable. This transition from imagination to realization could be measured and assessed. Ideal / real was like other dilemmas discussed in the Introduction, for example failure while simulating later corrected, discoveries later verified, disorder re-ordered.

But there was a further minimal requirement. This was, actually, a part of the ideal / real dilemma. Those being taught to innovate must be able to make distinctions between one idea and another, if only to select the most attractive. Indeed, the more distinctions they made, the better positioned they were to find a new, valuable combination. This was the purpose of the entrepreneurial ecosystem described in Chapter 2. But making many distinctions was not enough. Innovators had to *reconcile* or integrate at least some of those distinctions, the strange with the familiar, the old with the new, the part with the whole, the shock with the recognition, emotion with intellect etc. Hence in setting out to measure innovation we need distinctive ideas leading to realities which have reconciled two or more of those distinctions in a novel synthesis, as these ideas transit from shadow to substance.

Because we need respondents firstly to differentiate and secondly to integrate or reconcile the distinctions, our questionnaire places these two tasks in sequence. We first ask the respondent if his/her education has been realistic and then ask the same respondent whether his/her education has been idealistic. Note that asking the two questions in this way obliges the respondent to make an initial distinction between realism and idealism. Once this distinction has been mentally processed, it makes sense to ask whether the pedagogy allowed these two values to be *integrated*, so that ideals were actually realized.

To distinguish and measure the degree of realism compared with idealism we used a conventional Likert Scale, like this:

QUESTION X

Please indicate your judgement of the values attained by Nanyang Technological University (NTU) and Nanyang Technopreneurship Centre (NTC) as measured against the following statements.

(a) My education has been realistic. It readies me for the world as it is, not necessarily as it might be. It is practical and effective.

Not true at all								Very true indeed	
1	2	3	4	5	6	7	8	9	10

(b) My education has been idealistic. It shows me how realities can be changed, so as to create new values. It is inspirational.

Not true at all								Very true indeed	
1	2	3	4	5	6	7	8	9	10

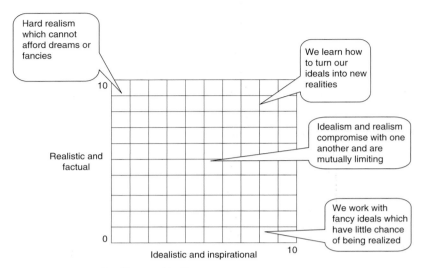

GRID 3.1 Realism vs. idealism

We have now measured realism and idealism within the pedagogy of the course separately, but we have not measured their degree of integration or reconciliation. To be innovative the ideal must become real and the distinction between the two needs to dissolve into a realized ideal.

In order to discover whether this has occurred we confront the respondent with Grid 3.1. 'Realistic' and 'factual' are on the vertical axis, 'idealistic' and 'inspirational' are on the horizontal axis. What the grid allows us to conceive is that the two axes have been integrated. We do this consistently throughout the questionnaire, making the traditional value more hierarchical by placing it on the vertical axis and the newer value more lateral on the horizontal axis, since it seeks equality with the traditional value. The grid allows us to see that realism can be attained at the expense of idealism at top left. Alternatively, idealism can be attained at the expense of realism at bottom right, or the two can clash in conflict in the middle of the grid. Yet it is also possible for the two to be reconciled at top right.

The pop-up balloons are there to guide the respondents' choices as to the degree or absence of integration. 'Hard realism which cannot afford dreams or fancies' is an example of realism crushing idealism. 'We work with fancy ideals with little chance of being realized' is precisely the counterfeit creativity complained of earlier in the chapter, a way of discovering fraudulence. 'Idealism and Realism compromise with one another and are mutually limiting' testifies to a conflict between these values. But 'we learn how to turn our ideals into new realities' is evidence of reconciliation. The closer to the top-right corner of the grid the respondent scores, the more innovative is that culture or ecosystem. What we are in search of is a pattern of integrated values.

Note that we did not retain the scores on the Likert Scales. These were simply an exercise to get the respondent to make a distinction, before seeing whether that distinction had been reconciled or not. We invited students to compare their earlier experiences as under-graduates, mostly at NTU, with their present experiences in the TIP course. We invited the participants in the Mandarin-speaking class in Shanghai to compare their TIP experiences with their undergraduate days in Chinese universities. We wanted to discover whether TIP was an improvement on their earlier educations or fell short in this regard. We especially wished to know whether, in a bid to make participants more innovative, TIP was sacrificing the traditional values of the university, as progressive educators are so frequently accused of doing.

But we need to look much more closely at what is happening at the top right of the grid where these seemingly 'opposed' values suddenly come together. At one moment they seem to be in conflict, the real crushing the ideal, the ideal attempting to subvert the real, and then all of a sudden they seem to melt into each other, the ideal becoming real while still retaining its idealism. It is a common-sense observation that many very realistic persons have no time for ideals, while many idealists seem to hide from the real world in convents, retreats, ivory towers, cults and sects. How can it be that values that typically assail each other politically and culturally, as when peace protestors put daisies in the barrels of rifles pointed towards them, can then suddenly become mutually supportive?

An answer was suggested in Abraham Marlow's seminal book *Motivation and Personality*.[3] While most psychologists and psychiatrists help the troubled and the sick, he examined lives that had been innovative, successful and fulfilled. He called these 'self-actualising persons', who became more fully themselves by fulfilling their own potentials. What he found among healthy subjects he then extended to the autobiographies and personal accounts of Americans who had made major contributions to sciences and the arts. Here is what he found, described in his own words.

> The age-old opposition between heart and head, reason and instinct, or cognition and conation was seen to disappear in healthy people where they became synergic rather than antagonists, and where conflict between them disappears because they say the same thing and point to the same conclusion ... The dichotomy between selfishness and unselfishness disappears ... because in principle every act is both selfish *and* unselfish. Our subjects are simultaneously very spiritual and very pagan and sensual. Duty cannot be contrasted with pleasure or work with play where duty *is* pleasure, when work *is* play ... Similar findings have been reached for kindness-ruthlessness, concreteness-abstractness, acceptance-rebellion, self-society, adjustment-maladjustment ... serious-humorous, Dionysian-Apollonian, introverted-extroverted, intense-casual, serious-frivolous ... mystic-realistic, active-passive, masculine-feminine, lust-love, Eros-Agape ... and a thousand philosophical dilemmas are discovered to have more than two horns, or paradoxically, no horns at all.[4]

What is fascinating about this passage is that the whole pattern of valuing shifts. It is not just two values that suddenly connect but whole sets of values. Could it be that when realism and idealism fuse they bring in their train a dozen or more other value differences so that distinctions and integrations, facts and inspirations, the strange and the familiar, old parts and new combinations also fuse?

Several other psychologists have made similar observations. Carl G. Jung wrote of the development of the 'true self' emerging from the midst of *coincidentia oppositorum*, a combination of seemingly contradictory forces.[5] He also pointed to 'synchronicity', an acausal process of spontaneous combination which yielded a new structure. He made much of symbols, from the Greek *sym-bol*, 'to throw together', and much of metaphors, the 'likeness of unlike characteristics'.

Carl Rogers wrote of the congruent personality developing out of congruent relationships.[6] Martin Buber spoke of the 'encounter on the narrow ridge' or the *insecurity* involved in *securing* another's affection. We can only find out if we are acceptable to another by risking the discovery that we are unacceptable. Our strength comes from making ourselves vulnerable.[7] Socrates was his hero because he insisted on dialogue and the values within us must engage in a similar dialogue.

A more recent contribution to the curious phenomenon of values ceasing to oppose and starting to conjoin is found in the work of Mihaly Csikszentmihalyi.[8] He began some years ago by researching into happiness and this is important because innovation can be intensely enjoyable. He asked respondents to keep diaries and record immediately following a very joyous experience everything they could remember. Such experiences were typically brief, intense and unforgettable. They departed as unexpectedly as they came. What was characteristic about them was the absorption of persons in an activity, often but not necessarily with other people. Csikszentmihalyi called these 'flow experiences' because categories appeared to collapse and oppositions melt. In sporting activities the skier became the piste, the swimmer the water, the player the ball. The problem-solver dissolves into the problem, sunk deep into its interstices, thrilled by its complexity.

Csikszentmihalyi asks us to imagine a team working on a complex project. The latter represents a challenge to the team, which brings to that challenge its assorted skills. A very common experience for team members is that the challenge is greater than their skills. In this event the team suffers from anxiety. They are about to be overwhelmed and their limitations will be exposed. But suppose the team's skills are

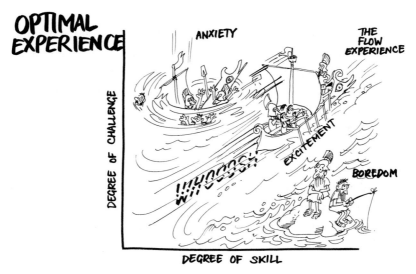

DIAGRAM 3.1

far greater than the challenge facing them? In this case they are likely to suffer boredom. This level of difficulty tests them not at all. They would prefer something more worthy of their powers. Diagram 3.1 shows the familiar conflict between challenges and skills, anxiety and boredom.

THE DILEMMA OF CHALLENGE VS. SKILL

But something quite unexpected and unusual happens in the case where skill and challenge are closely matched with each other. Instead of subtracting from one another, they augment one another. The challenge calls forth the skill, while the mounting skills actively seek more challenges. The boundaries between the two concepts dissolve into one whoosh of excitement in what Csikszentmihalyi calls a sense of 'flow' – see top right of the diagram. Anxiety and/or boredom have vanished in a great surge of energy.

In our view this happens also when ideals become realities, thereby fulfilling their idealism. Now you cannot tell the two apart because they flow together as one set of ideals realized, familiar parts combining to form a strange whole, yet somehow retaining aspects of familiarity, both shocking yet recognizable, new yet old. Abraham

Maslow spoke of 'oceanic experience', which has the same wave-like character.[9] It cannot be a coincidence that the word 'solution' means both an answer to our question and a liquid substance. It is as if we must turn from rocks of rectitude into flowing waves if we want to solve our problems and innovate. Existing 'hard' structures need to dissolve.

Edward de Bono in his book *Water Logic*[10] argues that we must escape from the 'object realm' of solid particles banging into each other, the world of Newton, and move into the 'frequency realm' of men like Clerk and Maxwell, with its waves of light, sound, magnetism and water. Perhaps objectivity is better reserved for dead physical objects not for live, organic creatures. The latter respond to us whether we are passionate or dispassionate. We discover our own shadows.

Working with another wave-like medium the psychologist Karl Pribram has likened the human brain to a hologram.[11] Since our brain cells emit electro-magnetic waves spontaneously, this is not far-fetched. In a hologram a laser beam that has encountered an object crosses a laser beam that is unaffected by it, and the waves intersecting carve out a three-dimensional image of what was seen, storing it in the striate cortex, the memory area of the brain that gives us vivid images.

When waves interact, rather like ripples on the surface of a pond, they are called 'interference waves'. This interference can be destructive so that they cancel each other out, like anxiety and boredom, or constructive so that they enhance one another, with higher peaks and lower valleys, known as amplitude. It can also produce complex, aesthetic patterns, waves within waves, variations on a theme as in music, so that the whole is much more than the parts. Abraham Maslow spoke of his creative subjects having 'peak experiences' as when two wave fronts elevate each other.[12]

It was William Blake who argued that 'contraries are positives'.[13] When they come together they heal and innovate. Anger and friendship, for example, interact to sustain relationships:

I was angry with my friend:
I told my wrath, my wrath did end.

I was angry with my foe:
I told it not, my wrath did grow.

When we love someone we almost inevitably hate some things about them, all the more because we hold them so dear. Loving others yet hating their faults and telling them this is how we socialize our children and influence each other.

Whether the world we inhabit consists of particles, tiny objects and atoms or of continuous waves of energy has divided physicists for years. Niels Bohr offered a Principle of Complementarity. The answer was both are true and this in turn depended on our own behaviour! If we used a particle detector we would discover particles. If we used a wave detector we would discover waves. Since the human brain is itself divided into left and right hemispheres, the first discrete and analytic, the second continuous and synthetic, it seems we have this choice within our own heads and will come up with opposed conclusions depending on which hemisphere is employed.[14] But there is also the *corpus callosum*, a bundle of nerves joining the right and left hemispheres. Could it be that in innovation the left hemisphere makes the initial distinction and the right hemisphere transcends these distinctions in a wave-like flow of energy? We need the whole brain to innovate, particles and waves, the real and the ideal.[15]

Another possible image for phenomena which interface with each other, either constructively or destructively, is a virtuous circle as opposed to a vicious circle. Since a wave *is* in fact a 'rolling circle', this is part of the same metaphor. Idealism can lose touch with reality and in its frustration push those ideals beyond any hope of realization. Similarly there are 'crack-pot realists' who argue that, because the atom bomb is real, we must junk our ideals, live in mineshafts if necessary and measure ourselves for radiation. These are both vicious circles in which one value dominates its contrasting value.

Alternatively where one's ideals are realized, more ideals will be forthcoming and more realization sought as the human condition is steadily improved. The ideal of civil rights and justice for black

Box 3.1   **The contrasting qualities of innovation according to multiple authorities**

The contrasts or dilemmas	Resolved or reconciled by ...	Author(s)
Yin vs. yang, primordial opposites	Everlasting movement of the Dao	The Tai Chi, authors unknown
Filial piety vs. personal conviction	'Remonstrate with your parents tactfully'	Confucius
Over-valuation of kinship vs. under-valuation	Oedipus myth showing excessive swings of the pendulum in tragic simulation, not reality	Sophocles interpretation by Lévi-Strauss (1979)
Dissent vs. loyalty	Dissenting in such a way that a new law can be made from manner of dissent	Socrates and Immanuel Kant
Collective unconscious vs. the libido	The developing 'self' integrating experience	Carl Gustav Jung (1971)
Coincidentia oppositorum	'The *enantiodromia* return swing of the pendulum'	Carl Gustav Jung
Primordial archetypes, i.e. Virgin Mother, crucified God and sacrificed Son	Symbolism, from Greek meaning 'throw together' and by 'synchronicity'	Carl Gustav Jung
Change in the affairs of cultures vs. continuity	Carried by the creative minority, decides fate of nations	Arnold Toynbee (1934–54)
Death wish vs. life wish	We create to defy our own mortality	Otto Rank interpreted by Ernest Becker (1973)
Luck or fortune vs. careful preparation	'Fortune favours the Prepared Mind'	Louis Pasteur

Creativity vs. destruction	Entrepreneurship is 'a gale of creative destruction'	J. A. Schumpeter (1975)
First-rate intelligence holds two opposed ideas in the mind …	… and still retains the capacity to function, e.g. hopelessness/ determination	F. Scott Fitzgerald
Violence vs. peacefulness	Non-violent action and demonstration	Mahatma Gandhi
Power vs. soul	'Soul power'	Martin Luther King (1963)
Change vs. freeze	Unfreeze–change–refreeze	Kurt Lewin (see Marrow 1969)
Selfish vs. unselfish conduct	A benign culture rewards selfless conduct to resolve dichotomy	Ruth Benedict (1934)
Myriad dichotomies: self–other, Eros–Agape, doubt–certainty …	… disappear and become synergic even as the self is actualized	Abraham Maslow (1954)
Two different matrices of thought …	… are 'bi-sociated' in the act of creation	Arthur Koestler (1964)
Strangeness vs. familiarity	Creativity makes the strange familiar and the familiar strange	William J. J. Gordon (1961)
Divergent thinking vs. convergent thinking, which symbolize the Arts and the Sciences	We first diverge to multiply options artistically, then converge scientifically	J. W. Getzels and P. W. Jackson (1962)
Vertical thinking vs. lateral thinking	These cross-connect in a 'water logic' of dissolved boundaries	Edward de Bono (1994)
Neurotic symptoms vs. high ego-strength	The capacity to rebound from purposeful risk-taking	Frank Barron (1968)
Reconstructed logic vs. the logic of discovery	Discovering first then verifying and codifying	Abraham Kaplan (1964)

Left brain vs. right brain	Joined by *corpus callosum* which connects the two	Roger W. Sperry (1964)
Experimentation vs. reflection, concrete vs. abstract	Experiment then reflect and move up and down abstraction ladder while learning	Donald Kolb (1985)
Normal science vs. paradigm change and revolution	Science proceeds normally until anomalous results spur paradigm change	Thomas Kuhn (1970)
Survival of the fittest vs. co-evolution	Survival of the 'fittingest', i.e. of those fitting best into their environments	Gregory Bateson (2000)
Mass production vs. customized products	Mass-produced components from which customized design is produced	Joe Pine (1993)
Model I: Behaviour in which the manager strives to win a conflict	Model II: Behaviour in which manager states view and invites inquiry into this	Chris Argyris (1986)
Designed strategy vs. emergent strategy	Crafted strategy is designed out of what has emerged	Henry Mintzberg (1989)
Finite games vs. infinite game	Learning from those who win is an infinite game	James P. Carse (1986)
The ability to play contrasts the real with the ideal and imagined	It is a mark of learning and civilization that we can imagine the tragic and the comic without suffering the consequences	John Huizinga (1970)
The global corporation vs. the multinational	The transcultural corporation integrates diverse resources	Christopher Bartlett and Sumantra Ghoshal (1991)

Seriousness vs. play	Be playful while you practise, simulate and rehearse, but your meeting with the market is serious	Michael Schrage (2000)
The Bourgeois vs. the Bohemian	Creative denizens of Silicon Valley unite the two styles	David Brooks (2001)
Leadership vs. innovation	Innovative leadership is like 'jamming' with an improvisational jazz group	John Kao (1996)
Tacit knowledge vs. explicit knowledge	Through an 'upward spiral' try to make the tacit explicit	Ikujiro Nonaka and Hirotaka Takeuchi (1995)
Supply innovation vs. demand innovation	Aim your supply at curing the customer's pain points	Adrian Slywotzky and Richard Wise (2003)
Challenges to a team vs. skills of that team	Usually subtract, but can combine in a *flow experience*	M. Csikszentmihalyi (1990)

Americans became enshrined in the Civil Rights Act, so that a black candidate can now be nominated for President, be taken seriously and win convincingly. This is a virtuous circle in which ideals spawn realities which motivate more ideals.

The truth of the matter is that the reconciliation of contrasting values or dilemmas has been a thread running through the work of many well-known thinkers. These themes are summarized in Box 3.1.

SUMMARY

Innovation is a veritable lexicon. We are determined to smoke out and expose pseudo-innovation, the fashionable pretence that one is creative just because one's conduct is bizarre. Whatever innovation may be it is falsified by stereotypes or clichés.

Innovation requires that we make numerous distinctions, at high levels of intensity. For instance, is China very capitalist but also very socialist? Can parts of a product be cheap but the whole valuable? Yet making distinctions is only the first step. Can these be successfully combined, e.g. market-driven socialism, low-cost yet high-value products? We designed our questionnaire so that respondents first made distinctions then told us whether these had been combined and integrated. We used a grid with pop-up balloons to prompt this choice, so that ideals would either be polarized with realism or ideals realized.

The process of integrating may need new waves of thinking, taken not from the 'object realm' of science but the 'frequency realm'. We have summarized the views of more than forty authors who have argued that contrasting values must be synthesized. We now turn to the list of questions, whose values were first distinguished then combined.

4 Co-defining innovative education: how the instrument was created

I have explained that for us the choice of ideals and their later combined realization defines entrepreneurship and innovation, but there are numerous variations upon this underlying theme. We chose eleven highly contrasting aims of education. Each of these included a traditional, realistic aim contrasted with a novel, idealistic aim, embodied within TIP itself. The traditional aims were important to Singapore's quest for a just meritocracy and the channelling of educational resources to the most able and studious. The entrepreneurial aims were essential to Singapore moving from followership to leadership, defining excellence for itself and then realizing this.

We were particularly concerned to discover whether encouraging students to be innovative might detract from or subvert the traditional canons of education. Entrepreneurs have not always been respectful of education. Henry Ford notoriously said that history is bunk. In the sixties and seventies extreme right-wing membership in the USA was found to correlate with 'status incongruence', that is high levels of commercial success but low educational levels. Senator Barry Goldwater, the American candidate for President, wanted to 'saw off the Eastern seaboard and have it float out to sea' with Harvard, Yale, Princeton and MIT graduates. Many supporters of entrepreneurs have been rabidly anti-intellectual. It has been said of those boasting that they are 'self-made men' that 'they relieve the Almighty of a heavy responsibility'. Was there a danger of TIP producing such characters?

This was an important question because Technopreneurship, as the Singapore government defined it, included the novel combination of high-tech resources. Persons hostile to education in any way would harm a society seeking to increase knowledge intensity. It was absolutely essential that respect for merit be maintained and not sacrificed.

In choosing what questions to ask, we were aware of the letters sent to the University President and to NTC, mostly praising the course (see Box 2.2). We wanted to know if these sentiments were isolated exceptions or widely shared. We already knew what principles went into designing the course – see Chapter 2 on the entrepreneurial ecosystem – and we were aware of several foundation pillars of education cited by the universities, including NTU. We wished to discover if these had been upheld or damaged. Finally we were aware of an extensive literature on creativity and innovation and were concerned to discover whether the hypotheses of these experts had been confirmed or confounded by our results.

In the list of values below the traditional values of the university and its realism are on the left while the novel values of the TIP and its idealism are on the right. For genuine innovation to occur, both sets of values must be strengthened and then combined at levels of high intensity. Pathology occurs whenever one end of a dichotomy militates against the other. Growth and learning occur when these combine in a 'flow state'.

Emphasized by universities (values of realism)	Emphasized by TIP (values of idealism)
1. Training the intellect to master and organize concepts	Training human experience, including feelings, emotions and ideals
2. Absorbing information given by instructors	Thinking for yourself and testing your convictions
3. Classroom culture resembles a level playing field for competitive efforts	Classroom culture resembles an extended family willing each other to succeed
4. Work is hard and serious, with long hours and hard challenges	Work is playful and enjoyable. The hours slip away as we are challenged
5. Career continuity and mastery are crucial	Transformation is vital. We re-invent ourselves

6. We learn to face facts, however discomforting, and report these objectively	We learn to develop mutual rapport so as to face together harsh facts and realities
7. We search for what is true and beautiful for the sake of those values	We pursue exciting aspirations leading to practical accomplishments
8. We learn rationality, scepticism, empiricism and how to verify notions	We learn to combine exciting ideas to generate notions worth verifying
9. We are taught to be humble before Nature and learn the laws that rule us	We are taught that Nature can be altered to change destinies boldly
10. Achievement is based on individual capability and how we compare with others	Achievement is based on team effort and how effective we are at engaging others
11. Merit is defined by authorities	Merit is defined by us and by clients

Our position was that the two columns should be mutually enhancing. For this to be accomplished we need 'a norm of equality' between them, with sufficient mutual respect to facilitate integration. Attempts to prioritize such values can do harm. They work together. I shall now go through these contrasts one by one, explaining why they were chosen.

I. TRAINING THE INTELLECT TO MASTER AND ORGANIZE CONCEPTS VS. TRAINING HUMAN EXPERIENCE, INCLUDING FEELINGS, EMOTIONS AND IDEALS

It is virtually impossible to innovate without being emotionally involved. In a very real sense the new product or service is you yourself, your dream, vision, imagination, gift and judgement. You stand to lose a lot more than money, although that can be distressing enough. Moreover you are venturing where few, if any, went before, staking your claim against the settled opinions of mankind. If no one wanted this before, why should they want it now? To say that a favourable response is uncertain is to put it mildly. Your heart is in your mouth. Your reputation has been wagered on the outcome. Your closest associates will soon know whether you are right or wrong and you may let them all down.

When one is in search of something new, feelings can be a good friend or a mortal enemy. There is a tendency to get excited, because, without realizing why, you are getting close. You need to trust your feelings and follow that excitement which like a Geiger counter zeroes in upon the hidden prize.

But while feelings run ahead of intellect, so that you get annoyed with a shoddy argument before you can explain its shoddiness, feelings are quite inaccurate. Not everything that excites you is true. The role of intellect is to monitor the reliability of those feelings, to test rigorously and dispassionately whether this is fool's gold or the genuine substance and to reconstruct intellectual concepts around your discovery so that these can be easily codified and communicated. Because emotion is inevitably strong, intellect must be at least as formidable and examine minutely what, if anything, you have captured.

We were much influenced by the work of Daniel Goleman on emotional intelligence.[1] Emotions do a lot of thinking for us, as when we meet someone we dislike and later discover how wise these feelings were. Research done by Diven (1937) discovered that we even generalize emotionally.[2] When an electric shock was administered twenty seconds after the word 'hay' was read out among a string of other words fewer than 10 per cent of respondents had realized this connection intellectually. But over 60 per cent showed increases in anxiety as soon as the word was mentioned again and 30 per cent generalized this anxiety to all words with rural connotations. This means our feelings even make classifications without our being consciously aware of it.

Those who do not trust their emotions are therefore unlikely to be able to follow a 'trail of excitement'. Those who have failed to develop a critical intellect will be unable to cross-examine their emotions to check their validity. The two faculties need each other for mutual support.

2. ABSORBING INFORMATION GIVEN BY INSTRUCTORS VS. THINKING FOR YOURSELF AND TESTING YOUR CONVICTIONS

We asked this question because of a well-known critique of Chinese pedagogy, that it emphasizes rote learning and memorized passages from Chinese classics, without requiring these to be challenged critically and selected or rejected by the learner.[3] We wanted to know if this tendency still characterized Singapore and the Chinese universities attended by members of our Mandarin-speaking class.

We were also aware that innovators bask in an 'excess' of information from which they choose concepts key to their convictions with which they are ready to run. Were they only to learn by rote they would fail entirely to differentiate themselves in the market-place and have nothing new to offer. On the other hand information has to come from somewhere and instructors are a ready source. There can be no objection to absorbing knowledge provided you process this actively and generate your own preferred synthesis.

The relationship between IQ and most creativity tests is a curious one. It is almost impossible to be creative without an IQ well above the average. Yet many 'brilliant' persons with stratospheric IQs can be almost entirely sterile. It is as if they spent their whole energies learning what other people expected them to know so that they could exhibit this. Being 'very clever' is an end in itself.[4]

3. CLASSROOM CULTURE RESEMBLES A LEVEL PLAYING FIELD FOR COMPETITIVE EFFORTS VS. CLASSROOM CULTURE RESEMBLES AN EXTENDED FAMILY WILLING EACH OTHER TO SUCCEED

We asked this question because Tan Teng-Kee regarded it as a crucial aspect of his programme and ecosystem design and because several students had remarked favourably on the 'family atmosphere' so unlike the educational environments encountered earlier. The intention was to make the projects pursued by members of the programme so diverse that head-to-head competition, of the kind that occurs for the highest grades, would be a process that was avoided, together with the enmity this generates. Everyone in the programme could succeed hugely without diminishing the success of others, since their feats were non-comparable.

That said, the 'Level Playing Field' has obvious merits and is a powerful metaphor. It is marked out clearly beforehand. It gives everyone a fair and equal chance to excel. It rewards merit and you get to discover where your relative strengths and weaknesses lie, so that you can hire talents that complement your own. Yet the Level Playing Field needs coaches, cheering sections and fans to keep competitors up to scratch. It is highly cooperative as well as competitive. The popularity of many of those who coach is legendary. These are persons who are on your side but who utilize that partisanship to criticize and make you even better. You can trust that the faults they find with your project are motivated by genuine concern for its future. Virtually all projects are improvable so that advice given to you by 'family' members on whose authenticity you can count assumes great importance in preparing you for the fray.

There is some evidence that 'friendly competition' or 'co-opetition' was present in golden ages of innovation. These were all very diverse and highly urbanized. In Athens the contest between playwrights to stage spectacular tragedies and comedies, paid for by profits from the silver mines, was intense. Yet the plays themselves celebrated *harmonia* and sent waves of shared emotion called *catharsis* through audiences. It is estimated that at the height of the Tan dynasty, China's golden age, there were 100,000 foreigners present in China and flourishing international trade along the Silk Road. After several massacres of foreigners the great age of innovation came to an abrupt end.[5]

Michelangelo, Galileo and his family all boarded with and shared households with their Medici sponsors in fifteenth- and sixteenth-century

Florence, the children of several families playing together. It is rare to find rich bankers fiercely dedicated to art and science, but when this happens a rare combination produces some rare results![6]

The Quakers and Nonconformists who helped to create Britain's industrial revolution had very close family-style relationships within their small sects, along with pledges always to keep their promises, 'my word is my bond'. Their relationships were unusually egalitarian. Quakers had women coordinate their meetings and tithed their members to educate apprentices.[7]

4. WORK IS HARD AND SERIOUS, WITH LONG HOURS AND HARD CHALLENGES VS. WORK IS PLAYFUL AND ENJOYABLE. THE HOURS SLIP AWAY AS WE ARE CHALLENGED

We asked this question because Michael Schrage's seminal work *Serious Play* had influenced the design of the course, because 'have fun' was very much our guiding principle and because students of Chinese background had to overcome their reticence and modesty to publicly aspire and drum up support.[8]

At first blush entrepreneurship and innovation are deadly serious. You are heading for a rendezvous with the market-place and the odds are not in your favour. You could lose everything for want of small details. It looks like a recipe for obsessive-compulsive disorder! Yet playfulness and enjoyment are quite essential for reasons touched on earlier. Mistakes are not serious if you learn from them and the errors are only simulated. Since you are practising something new and exciting you might as well enjoy yourself. Since your project aims to bestow new satisfactions upon customers you should embody those satisfactions in advancing your project. Since the innovative project is for the time being imaginary and visionary you need to project the happy state of affairs which the fulfilment of your dream brings about. Entrepreneurship is in part a self-fulfilling prophecy, so enjoy that prospect, share its enjoyment and persuade allies to bring it about. Comedy has a way of averting tragedy. Learn to laugh at your false starts and your more absurd conjectures and you are less likely to weep at the final outcome when all resources have been expended. We learn very rapidly when we play. Your chief hope is that you have learned sufficiently fast to make your finished project a winner.[9]

We were particularly interested in the phrase 'the hours slip away', since Csikszentmihalyi had noticed the 'collapse of time' in happy moments of intense enjoyment when absorbed in problem-solving.[10] We hoped to find support for this.

5. CAREER CONTINUITY AND MASTERY ARE CRUCIAL VS. TRANSFORMATION IS VITAL. WE RE-INVENT OURSELVES

Here we were very conscious that most Singaporean graduates emerge from university with degrees which are the keys to their later careers. They have been educated to specialize, sometimes quite narrowly. Yet teaching them to innovate is going to lead them across the boundaries of that career and speciality into other careers and other specialities, the combination of which can be transformative. We were very conscious of Alvin Toffler's dictum that most innovative breakthroughs now occur rather in the spaces between disciplines.[11]

We were concerned with two possibilities, that narrowness of career specialization might militate against transformation and that those who experienced being transformed by the TIP programme might lose the mastery of the career they had chosen earlier. Both these outcomes would be undesirable and TIP might be doing harm.

Transformation-of-self is in some danger of becoming 'psycho-babble' and encouraging self-indulgence. So we sought assurance that participants had not let go of the basic discipline which until the TIP programme had shaped their lives and made them employable. If they could transform themselves while still mastering their discipline, we believed that this change would be more authentic.

6. WE LEARN TO FACE FACTS, HOWEVER DISCOMFORTING, AND REPORT THESE OBJECTIVELY VS. WE LEARN TO DEVELOP MUTUAL RAPPORT SO AS TO FACE TOGETHER HARSH FACTS AND REALITIES

There are at least two sources of resilience in the face of negative feedback from your environment. The first is the traditional value of objectivity. Facts are facts and your wish that these were otherwise is not germane. You must learn to confront them without blinking. Reality is as it is, not as we would like it to be. The innovator must steel herself against disappointment because there is going to be plenty of it.

Yet we wondered whether traditional objectivity, although valuable, was enough. Customers' desires may be subjective and not lend themselves easily to factual analysis. Moreover, dispassion and the detachment of the objective observer is simply not present in most entrepreneurs and innovators. They are passionately attached to their projects and could not persevere so long if this were not so.

We therefore anticipated that their courage to face bad news and their readiness to improve their project came less from 'objectivity' than the rapport and support they received from team members and from the family atmosphere of the programme. We were also concerned to establish that their sense of objectivity and its importance as a discipline had not been subverted by the 'can do' enthusiasm engaged among fellow participants. We wanted to see traditional values upheld.

7. WE SEARCH FOR WHAT IS TRUE AND BEAUTIFUL FOR THE SAKE OF THOSE VALUES VS. WE PURSUE EXCITING ASPIRATIONS LEADING TO PRACTICAL ACCOMPLISHMENTS

We continued to worry about whether there was something inherently vulgar about entrepreneurship and innovation. We were mindful of Matthew Arnold's hymn to Oxford University as 'an adorable dreamer and haven from the purely practical'. When we do something not for its own sake, but to serve a utilitarian purpose and generate money, are we losing contact with the true value of education which is to awaken us to truth and beauty, pursued for their own sakes and not just for their saleability? However desirable it might be to become more innovative, we should be aware of the price paid. Might erosion occur in a university's commitment to eternal verities? Might these be twisted out of shape by commercial interests?

While there is reason to believe that this could happen, there were other reasons to believe it might not. Are we ever more authentically human than when we put our ideals at risk to create what was not there before? Is not genuine truth and real beauty something we make for ourselves, not something produced by a genius safely dead and foisted upon us by an art gallery? Is there a more precious endowment than knowing we are a source of value?

8. WE LEARN RATIONALITY, SCEPTICISM, EMPIRICISM AND HOW TO VERIFY NOTIONS VS. WE LEARN TO COMBINE EXCITING IDEAS TO GENERATE NOTIONS WORTH VERIFYING

In this question we were very conscious of a distinction made by the philosopher of science, Abraham Kaplan. He pointed out the difference between Reconstructed Logic, the way knowledge is verified, codified and passed on to the next generation, and the Logic of Discovery, how innovations actually occur amid mess, accident and noise.[12] Logic and rationality depend on correct classification. 'Men are mortal. Socrates is a man, therefore Socrates is mortal.' But innovation alters existing classifications and hence is irrational according to old classifications.

The TIP course concentrated very much on the Logic of Discovery, but might this weaken allegiance to rationality, scepticism, empiricism and verification? We very much hoped not. After all, a new discovery or product design needs to be verified and codified before the customers can properly use it. Innovators must both create and verify that their creation is useful. An attitude of scepticism ('Show me!') is very useful in this regard. The product either works as it was supposed to or does not. Whatever messiness and accident characterizes discovery should not be allowed to contaminate a thoroughly tested product. Once again we were searching for high scores on both criteria.

9. WE ARE TAUGHT TO BE HUMBLE BEFORE NATURE AND LEARN THE LAWS THAT RULE US VS. WE ARE TAUGHT THAT NATURE CAN BE ALTERED TO CHANGE DESTINIES BOLDLY

Some of the archetypal stories of mankind concern the Mad Scientist, The Sorcerer's Apprentice, the Faustian pact with the Devil which confers earthly powers at the price of your immortal soul, and Frankenstein's Monster – ostensibly the final act of creation, but in fact an ugly juxtaposition of body parts crudely stitched together in a mockery of Divine Creation, a lonely monster doomed to rage and despair. The common theme in all these stories is that we have heedlessly tinkered with the natural world which God gave us and brought calamity upon ourselves. We must be much more humble before Nature and learn the laws that rule us before trying to intervene.

Modern universities have indeed tried to do this, giving us a vision of a Great Perpetual Motion Machine hovering in space and moving on inexorably, entirely indifferent to our impotent desires and tiny strength. E.A. Burtt has suggested that this bleak view of the universe has been too prominent and has killed our creative spirit. The protests of the sixties and early seventies were in part a repudiation of this desolate landscape. He wrote movingly that Man had been reduced 'to a puny, irrelevant spectator imprisoned in a dark room. The world that people had thought they were living in – a world rich in colour and sound, redolent with fragrances – speaking everywhere of purposeful harmony and creative ideals – was crowded now into minute corners in the brains of scattered organic beings. The really important world outside was a world cold, hard, colourless, silent and dead.'[13]

At first scientists feared to examine the mind. The Soul belonged to God. But with much of secularism they got around to examining the mind itself, and unsurprisingly they viewed it as just another machine, one in subjection to the Great Machine. To innovate we must find the courage to tinker with it.

10. ACHIEVEMENT IS BASED ON INDIVIDUAL CAPABILITY AND HOW WE COMPARE WITH OTHERS VS. ACHIEVEMENT IS BASED ON TEAM EFFORT AND HOW EFFECTIVE WE ARE AT ENGAGING OTHERS

We were convinced that without team intervention most creative ideas come to nothing. A single person in a corporation talking up his/her pet idea is very likely to be ignored and eventually told to shut up, a reason, if one were needed, why corporations so seldom re-create themselves. A team is needed to champion an idea, to shape it, propose it loudly and forcibly produce a working prototype, improve it and push it through to final completion. Unless teams are sponsored and encouraged to champion new projects these will run into the sand. Yet university education generally constricts itself almost entirely to assessing individuals and attributing to them all credit for what they know. Indeed if you reveal in your essay that you might have learned something from your peers you may be accused of plagiarism. Echoing your teacher is OK. Echoing class-mates is not!

While we were confident that it was essential that team-work be taught to would-be innovators, we worried that this could lessen personal accountability. After all, if the group as a whole erred, might not each member escape personal blame? 'Group-Think' has been seen as the villain of many disasters. On the other hand, being socially skilful and persuasive might be one of the major resources of individuality. We were interested in discovering if teams and individuals could develop together. We hypothesized that this could happen.

11. MERIT IS DEFINED BY AUTHORITIES VS. MERIT IS DEFINED BY US AND BY CLIENTS

We asked this question because it loomed so large in the culture of Singapore. I argued in Chapter 1 that the nation's wealth had come largely by playing host to foreign corporations and practising 'catch-up capitalism'. In this process you let Americans define what is important and chase after the same standards so that it will be convenient for MNCs to locate in Singapore and train Singaporeans.

In order to be truly innovative it was necessary to *re-define merit and excellence* for yourself and then set forth to attain this. Your judges would be customers and consumers, not only those in top positions in the nation. Once customers had responded enthusiastically, authorities could be won over to *your* definition of merit. We wanted to know if pleasing authorities was preventing members of the English- or Mandarin-speaking programme from pleasing customers and themselves, or whether re-defining merit was damaging respect for authority. We believed both could be reconciled so as to grow together.

Let us now move on to the results of our survey.

5 The Singapore results

Before we detail the results of our assessment of this programme, let us consider whether asking our respondents to compare their undergraduate studies with this programme was a question that was remotely fair. Did we deliberately tilt the odds in our own favour? Is the comparison we asked for valid?

There are some reasons for suspecting bias towards TIP. Firstly, the TIP experience was more recent and might loom larger in the memories of respondents. Secondly, this was post-graduate education, ostensibly 'higher' than what had gone before. Thirdly, might they not be thanking a popular teacher? But it is the fourth objection that is perhaps the most probing. In boosting the confidence of respondents and instilling excitement and raised expectations were we not simply fishing for compliments? Were we simply measuring the heady enthusiasm we had ourselves encouraged? Perhaps, but it seems very unlikely. The 2002 class had been out in the cold for five years, the 2003 class for four years, and so on. Even the 2007 class had cooled their heels for several months before we asked them to respond. If indeed we had rendered them 'high' on extravagant dreams, then all concerned had had several months and up to five years to sober up and realize just how hard it is to innovate in a country with many safe multinational job opportunities. You can give students a 'high' without much difficulty but then you face their misery when they come down from that experience and must face reality.

The failure rate for entrepreneurial projects worldwide is estimated to be around 90 per cent. The likelihood that persons who responded to our research had tasted failures or at least set-backs was very high. What would be more natural than that they would blame the programme for any difficulty? Then there were those who needed a job and had to settle, at least temporarily, for uninspiring roles, since TIP fitted very few job classifications. Might we not expect a backlash against a programme that had promised so much? Those who generate false optimism tend to get clobbered and rightly so. Out there in the Singaporean environment you mostly do as you are told!

What about the accusation that our respondents simply gave a popular teacher the positive evaluation that they knew he was looking for? Well, if he had disappointed them when they ventured forth armed with his advice, surely they would not hesitate to disappoint him? The programme was all about facing the truth in cases where your project was defective. Had the course been defective surely they would have told him frankly. They owed him that at least. They had been told repeatedly, 'You learn from *negative* feedback.' It is hard to believe they would spare their teachers what they had so often been told was right for them.

As for the superiority of post-graduate education, it is rather the reverse. It is undergraduate years that are remembered with nostalgia and that open the purse strings of alumni years later. The difficulty graduate schools have in tapping into the same largesse is notorious. Undergraduate courses last three to four years and you have the option of electing your favourite subjects and teachers towards the end. When you graduate you have a career opened up before you and a higher degree. You may even excel in your favourite sport. In contrast, TIP lasts only four months. It borrows fame from no graduate school. You cannot elect courses. You cannot choose preferred teachers. You receive only a diploma and instead of a safe, settled career, you are offered a maelstrom of opportunities and criss-crossing trajectories. Nor is NTU a university whose undergraduate programmes are weak. It is among the top half-dozen schools in East Asia and around seventieth in world league tables. Doing better than NTU's undergraduate courses would be no easy task.

So, far from any bias in this survey being in TIP's favour, it would seem more probable that it would be the other way around. An engineer two or three years out of college would probably thank his university for an auspicious start to his career. It was his/her university that provided a discipline-for-life. But would entrepreneurs be equally grateful, after the bruising experience they almost certainly encountered? It seems unlikely. The case of the Mandarin-speaking class in Shanghai is even more open to negative bias. They would have to admit that a class designed and taught mostly by immigrants from Southern China – not the most prestigious region of the country – had outperformed their chosen national universities. We could understand their hesitation.

If there is a bias in this survey, and we have done our best to minimize it, then respondents are more likely to value their undergraduate years of education, with their promise of abiding friendships, secure futures and global assessments. The brief, frenetic pace of the programme on innovation would have to work very hard to compete. Were TIP to show even a slight improvement on education-as-usual then this would be remarkable. But as we shall see, the improvement was anything but slight.

THE RESULTS

We now turn to the evaluation of TIP as compared to NTU undergraduate courses. We found 153 qualified respondents. Many others had attended other universities. These were omitted. Many qualified respondents were out of the country and pre-occupied with business. We received 68 usable replies. All questions were on the theme of Realism vs. Idealism. We regarded the first as a traditional value, which NTU was pledged to uphold. We regarded the second 'progressive' value as one essential to innovation and acclaimed by TIP and many creativity experts.

We first used the Likert scale to measure from 1 to 10 how *intellectual* the pedagogy was in the mastery and organization of key ideas. We next used the same scale to measure how *experiential* the pedagogy was, in working with feelings and emotions. Respondents were then presented with Grid 5.1 and were asked to locate themselves upon it.

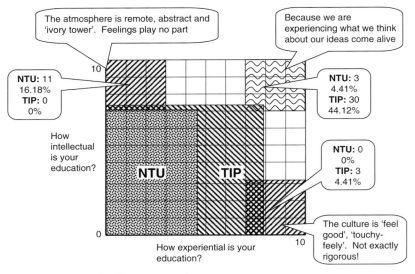

GRID 5.1 Intellect vs. experience

They did not have to copy straight from their earlier scores, although they might do so. We were looking for those who could experience emotionally what they were thinking about, as indicated at the top right of the grid. We were also looking for those who failed in this attempt, at top left and bottom right, or who compromised in the middle. To this end pop-up balloons prompted their choices and nudged them to consider whether these values had been integrated.

DILEMMA I INTELLECTUAL ORDERING
VS. EMOTIONAL EXPERIENCE

The responses are set out in Grid 5.1 and we see that 'Prof. Tan' and his TIP education has not only exceeded other university courses, but has done so by landslide proportions. This is not on one axis only, as we might have supposed, but on both. If you use your intellect to be innovative not only do you have your heart in your mouth, you strive to be more rigorously intelligent still, since your whole future now depends upon it. Although vivid emotional experiences can detract from intellectual rigour and although intellectual activity at universities often occurs in a moratorium from stressful experiences, intellect and experience can develop together. This is strongly suggested by TIP's scores as shown in this grid.

The different locations on grids 5.1–5.11 need to be explained. There are two 'pathology zones', the nine squares at top left and the nine at bottom right. There is one 'reconciliation zone', the wavy pattern across the nine squares at top right. The average scores for the NTU pedagogy are clearly marked as are the average scores for the TIP pedagogy taught at NTC. In virtually all cases the number of squares occupied by TIP is substantially greater than the number occupied by NTU. We see that the intellectual attainment in the 'Technopreneurship' course was judged to have exceeded the NTU average. The TIP course scored 7.20 out of 10, compared to the university average of 7.06. Yet, as expected, TIP won hands down on the intensity of emotional experience, scoring 7.97 to the university's 4.78. The simplest comparison is to count the number of squares covered in Grid 5.1 by NTU and by TIP. When we do this NTU covers 33.26 squares and TIP 57.38: the latter is 74.2% higher ($R2 = 34.23\%$, $P < 0.01$).

We laid two deliberate traps for TIP and the university respectively. These are represented by the 'pathology zones' top left and bottom right. We prompted respondents to say that the TIP programme was 'feel good' and 'touchy feely', see bottom right of the diagram. We wanted to smoke out any anti-intellectualism. But only 4.41% agreed with this verdict. We also prompted respondents to say that NTU courses were 'Abstract, ivory tower and remote'. Fully 16.18% agreed that this was so (see Appendix II). It is important to stress that NTU as a university does succeed on its own terms. 42.65% of its students rated their education as 8, 9 or 10 on intellectuality (see Appendix III). What it does not do so well is to bring intellectual order to its own personal experiences. Only 4.41% of respondents scored their undergraduate learning in the 'reconciliation zone' (the wavy square at top right), while 44.12% of TIP graduates reached this zone, their 'ideas coming alive'. Hence on Dilemma 1, TIP's capacity to combine intellectuality with emotion, the programme scores ten times higher.

DILEMMA 2 ABSORBING INFORMATION TOP-DOWN
VS. THINKING AND DOING FROM BOTTOM-UP

Our second dilemma, one that affects all pedagogy, is to consider how learning is communicated. Is it transmitted top-down by educators 'filling up' students with information and knowledge? This was the view of John Locke, that educators 'wrote' upon the *tabula rasa* of the mind. Or are there innate structures of the mind (Platonic forms) that educators elicit, so that in a sense we already know? Clearly both visions have some validity. Those who wish to think and act for themselves need information with which to think and they might be wise to listen first, or they may jump to a wrong conclusion. Those who only absorb conventional wisdoms filtering down upon them may take on the characteristics of a sponge. Since this accusation had been made against traditional Chinese education,[1] we wished to see if it had lingered. Genuine innovation requires us not just to listen and absorb, but to select, convince ourselves and act. We obtained the results shown in Grid 5.2.

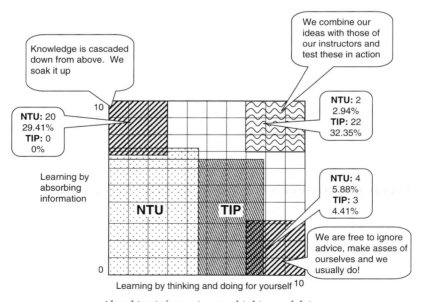

GRID 5.2 Absorbing information vs. thinking and doing.

Once again the pathologies are cross-hatched at top left and bottom right, while the wave-forms characteristic of the reconciliation zone are top right. Comparing the number of squares covered gives NTU a score of 33.66 and TIP a score of 53.52 squares covered. This is a 60% advantage ($R2=25.36\%$, $P<0.01$). As we had anticipated NTU scored higher on the top-down transmission of knowledge, but the difference was surprisingly small, considering how much less time TIP spends lecturing, compared to the university at large. NTU scored 7.24 and TIP 6.74. Anyone wishing to think and act using information would need first to absorb the information. It seems TIP students did this. When it came to 'thinking and acting for oneself', the university scored only 4.66 and was swamped by TIP scoring 7.94, almost three squares higher. Again we tested the authenticity of 'thinking and acting' for oneself. Was it just pretending? We prompted the answer 'We are free to ignore advice, make asses of ourselves and we usually do!' Yet only 5.88% taxed TIP with this fault. We prompted respondents to complain of NTU that 'Knowledge is cascaded down from above. We soak it up'. 29.41% believed this to be the case, so the concerns about passive memorization are upheld.

The university succeeds in its aims with 58.82% testifying that information from above is absorbed in the degrees of 8, 9 and 10 (Appendix III), yet only 2.94% felt that they could use that information to think for themselves! In contrast 32.35% of TIP scored in the reconciliation zone by absorbing information and also using it to think (see Appendix IV).

DILEMMA 3 COMPETING ON THE LEVEL PLAYING
FIELD VS. COOPERATING IN AN EXTENDED FAMILY
Whether business enterprise is 'basically' competitive or cooperative is one of the oldest arguments. But no one witnessing the rise of Asian countries with Confucian family-based ethics can doubt that familial relationships play an important part. The case is even stronger for creativity and innovation. Great writers, artists and scientists, for the most part, knew and respected each other and were members of a salon

or group. Creative eras tend to come in bursts of one or two generations. There occurs an inter-stimulation of like minds, a mixing of intimate strangers. There are signs of this today in such places as Amsterdam, Seattle, the Bay Area, Helsinki, Dublin, Taipei and Shanghai.

Singapore follows the American 'level playing field' axiom, so faithfully that it may be a purer meritocracy than its mentor. Yet innovation is crucially different because exactly what constitutes 'merit' has not been defined beforehand. You need an extended family of colleagues to champion and to give significance to what you are trying to do, which authorities may not recognize. It may be recalled that we wanted to test the proposition that where those in the class wanted something different from each other, head-on rivalry would be less and most would wish each other well. We believed a 'family' of innovators might well rejoice at each other's fortune. Players needed coaches. Might programme members willingly coach one another, mixing cold criticism of the work with warm support for the person?

It was, at any rate, our hypothesis that TIP might be both more competitive and also more cooperative and familial than NTU. We believed this to be true of creative communities historically, a crucial blend of personal striving with interpersonal supportiveness, a co-mingling of contrasting minds.[2] See Grid 5.3 for the results.

NTU covered in all 26.80 squares. TIP covered 56.37, or 103% higher ($R2 = 36.23\%$, $P < 0.01$). TIP's average score on competitiveness was 7.19, compared to 6.85 for NTU, so that NTC was even more competitive than the mean for the university at large; but on the classroom environment resembling an extended family the university scored only 4.22 compared with TIP's 7.84, a huge margin of 3.62. Once again the university 'succeeds' in being competitive, 42.65% score the environment 8, 9 or 10 as a 'level playing field' for competition, yet 44.12% of TIP respondents report 'co-opetition', with competition and cooperation in a family-style culture reconciled at top right. Once again we probed for dysfunctional extremes of too much familial atmosphere and too much 'cut-throat' competition (see cross-hatched

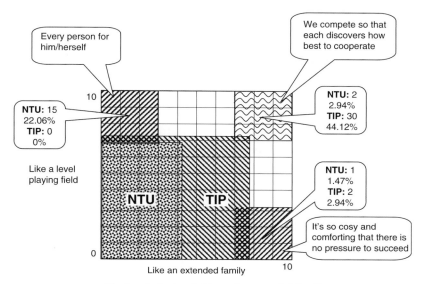

GRID 5.3 The level playing field vs. the extended family

squares). We tempted respondents to admit that the family atmosphere at TIP was 'cosy, comforting and free of pressure', but only 2.94% agreed. We also tempted respondents to say that NTU's competitiveness placed 'Every person for him/herself' and 22.06% agreed – a rather worrying proportion. NTU appears to have imported a large dollop of Western-style alienation into its pedagogy. Undergraduates feel apart, absorbing information with their emotions not engaged.

DILEMMA 4 SERIOUS HARD WORK VS. PLAYFUL ENJOYMENT

Those who want to succeed in the world of free enterprise and opportunities-for-all had best take such challenges seriously. Few will make it without determination and perseverance. Hard work is the inescapable recipe. Yet countless studies of innovative persons note their playfulness. They have created something that gives them untold pleasure and they want to share it. They find joy in their work and are guided by secret delights. Moreover, much use is made of simulations, skits, role plays, prototypes and models, because these can fail inexpensively. Innovators practise with 'toys' as the actual product takes shape.[3]

Michael Schrage[4] has suggested that innovation consists of Serious Play, i.e. a playful process leading to a serious outcome, light-hearted experimentation in search of a crucial solution. We hypothe-sized that the university would tend towards seriousness, even to the point of strenuousness. We knew TIP was much more playful, but were its participants aware of the serious purpose? The course has a business simulation running its full length. It has practice presentations to Venture Capitalists and many skits and plays, but were these games more than fun? Could seriousness and playfulness combine in a joyful rendezvous with reality? Could playful prototypes culminate in seri-ous products and services? Could we take the problems seriously but not ourselves? Play inevitably involves error, but because models, simulations and prototypes are cheap, such errors are not 'serious' as much as instructive. Piet Hein calls it 'The Road to Wisdom'.

> The road to wisdom – well, it's plain
> And simple to express:
> Err and err and err again
> But less and less and less.[5]

What we are talking about is the 'error correcting system'.

As we see in Grid 5.4, the university scored 7.54 on seriousness, but interestingly TIP is extremely close behind with 7.50, a non-significant margin. TIP is quite as serious as NTU. But when it comes to playfulness the difference is dramatic. The university scored 4.24 on playfulness and TIP scored 7.97, over three squares more. NTU covered 31.54 squares and TIP 59.78, or 91% higher ($R2=34.53\%$, $P<0.01$).

We tested to see whether TIP's playfulness was 'like a non-stop party', a trap it is easy to fall into, but only 4.41% agreed. We asked if the experience of university courses was not 'a bit grim and strenuous' and 22.06% agreed. Once again TIP has demonstrated that playful processes can prepare for serious purposes, as the hours slip by because

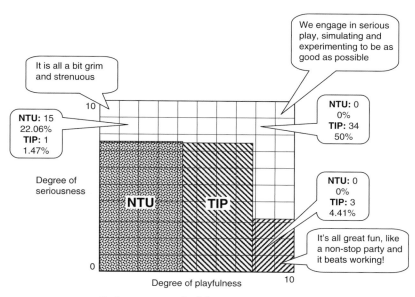

GRID 5.4 Seriousness vs. playfulness

you are enjoying yourself. 50.00% of respondents said that TIP reconciled work and play, but none (0%) claimed that the university managed this.

But note that once again the university succeeds on its own terms. 52.94% of its students score the teaching environment 8, 9 or 10 in seriousness, even if fun is scarce. However, this is lower than TIP's score on playfulness.

DILEMMA 5 CAREER CONTINUITY AND MASTERING
CHOSEN PATH VS. TRANSFORMATION OF YOURSELF
AND RE-INVENTION

Universities still prepare people for careers, although how long certain careers can now last grows ever more problematical. Whole technologies may come to the end of their useful lives. Nevertheless, continuity remains crucial, as does choosing your career path. Even innovations tend to advance certain disciplines and callings, with one innovation forming the 'platform' on which the next is based and so on. The core competence of a company makes no sense without thematic continuities.

Increasingly those who learn will ride a new technology for perhaps five to ten years and then transform and re-invent themselves, jumping from one form of competence to a contiguous one in variations on underlying themes. The TIP course was designed to help students transform themselves, hopefully without losing an underlying sense of continuity. Is it possible to combine the two, changing radically while still retaining a stable identity? We believe it is. Transformation that sacrifices continuity takes you back to square one. In any true development there must be a path, however winding, that brings you to your destination.

We set out to discover how NTU and TIP balanced career continuity with self-transformation of the kind that outstanding entrepreneurs and innovators achieve. We expected NTU to stress continuity and TIP to stress transformation, but we hoped to discover whether TIP retained at least some sense of continuity, without which a sense of growth and the development of core capabilities over time may be lost. Knowledge is to an important extent cumulative. One verified proposition links to another. We generalize as far as we can and then examine the exceptions. Disrupt continuity and you break up knowledge into incoherent fragments. TIP must serve both continuity and transformation. What 'technopreneurship' means is that you simultaneously follow relevant technologies in their most advanced states, yet take a stand between these. As we shall see, TIP succeeded in this. You take the most advanced work from at least two disciplines and create a novel synthesis between them. Grid 5.5 shows how they scored.

NTU covered 34.80 squares. TIP covered 49.45 or 67% higher ($R2 = 24.77\%$, $P < 0.01$). NTU outscores TIP on career continuity by 7.76 to 6.81 or 0.95. Note how small this difference is and how emphatic is the TIP course on maintaining a sense of continuity. Since innovations often combine two disciplines, the entrepreneur needs to be aware of career trajectories that are converging or running parallel in a way that makes connections possible. The combination of two lines is often transformative, while still retaining the initial continuities.

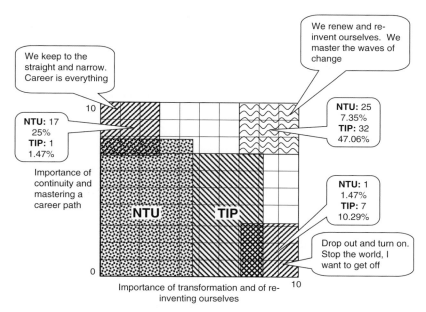

GRID 5.5 Career continuity vs. periodic transformation

When we asked how transformative NTU's courses were, the university scored 4.69 but TIP scored 8.35, nearly four squares better. 47.06% of respondents reported that TIP combined continuity with transformation (the reconciliation zone), but only 7.35% made that claim for NTU. We checked that TIP was not cheating by selling transformation as 'dropping out and turning on' Hippie fashion, but 10.29% agreed that it was, and there may be a little danger here. We asked whether students 'kept to the straight and narrow' at NTU and 25% agreed. Yet this 'straightness' meant that 63.24% of our respondents rated the university at 8, 9 and 10.

DILEMMA 6 HARD OBJECTIVITY VS. NEGATIVE FEEDBACK AMID RAPPORT

Here we were concerned with two different ways of confronting realities which are sometimes disagreeable. The science education given by universities insists on objectivity, at looking at hard facts without

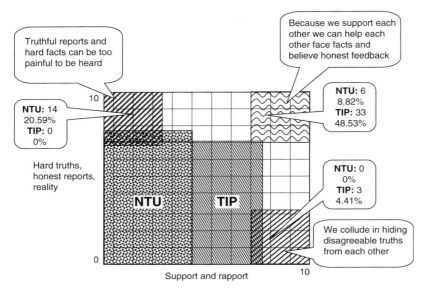

GRID 5.6 Hard objectivity vs. negative feedback amid rapport

blinking and steeling oneself to the truth, however unwelcome. The education given by those who would teach innovation emphasizes facing negative feedback (what you did not expect) and giving such feedback to each other in the context of rapport and mutual assistance.

These are different but not mutually exclusive ways of confronting harsh reality. The world is not always as we would like it to be. Our 'brilliant' inventions may not be wanted in their present condition. We suspected that innovators could well use both these ways of engaging the world, but that conventional science education would emphasize only the first. The scores shown in Grid 5.6 confirm our hypotheses.

The 'squares test' gives NTU 33.60 and TIP 57.62, a difference of 70% (R2 = 25.13%, P < 0.01). The university scored 7.82 for facing hard facts, only marginally above TIP at 7.07. The difference is 0.75. It is clear that both seek to face objective facts and that the university's emphasis upon this is largely to the exclusion of other forms of courage. We say this because mutual rapport and facing authentic, negative feedback from those close to you is much more pronounced in TIP; the university scored 4.53 on this and TIP 8.15, a difference of 3.62. The reasons a product does not fly may not always be 'objective'. The customers' preferences may be elusive. The path to understanding, as opposed to objective appraisal, is through authentic feedback, constructively communicated. We need the innovator to keep trying!

We looked to see if either of these ethics had been corrupted. Those who rely on negative feedback from persons in close rapport may 'collude in hiding disagreeable truths from each other'. We found 4.41% of the respondents believing this happened in TIP. This gives the programme no reason to worry. Yet those who claim to look at cold facts 'objectively' may find these 'too painful to face'. 20.59% of the replies indicated that this was the case in other university courses. 48.53% of respondents claimed that TIP taught them both kinds of courage, but only 8.82% attributed this to NTU. That both kinds of courage may be required to advance science has been suggested by Thomas Kuhn.[6]

DILEMMA 7 PURE QUEST FOR KNOWLEDGE
VS. KNOWLEDGE FOR PRACTICAL USE

We were determined not to slant our questions so that the university would lose. The issue above puts the university in the best possible light while equating TIP only with what is practical, useful and effective, hardly equivalent to truth and beauty! We wanted to see by how wide a margin the university might beat TIP, although even beautiful truths need to be effectively and knowledgeably used. One of the most venerable missions of the university is to pursue truth wherever it leads, whether such directions are 'useful' or not. In comparison, TIP is concerned with what works, surely a less elevated aim? Entrepreneurship is widely regarded as a non-academic subject, something akin to conjuring, performed by persons of somewhat suspect origins, often immigrants! On the other hand, innovative persons can ill afford a cavalier attitude to truth and beauty. In creating, creation is frequently an inspiration. What exists is the building blocks from which the new emerges.

As we see in Grid 5.7, NTU covered 41.78 squares and TIP 56.06, a 27% difference ($R2 = 7.26\%$, $P < 0.01$). So we find that an attempt to

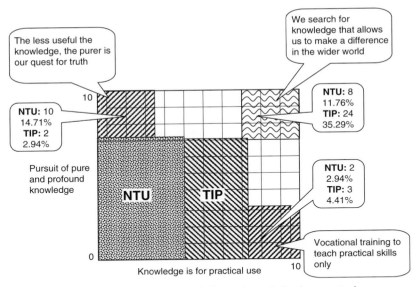

GRID 5.7 Pure quest for knowledge vs. knowledge for practical use

put TIP in its place, somewhere beneath the truth and beauty pursued by the university at large, was barely successful. The university scored 7.22 and TIP, a programme with no pretensions to teaching either value, scored 7.06, only 0.16 beneath. Perhaps we need truth and beauty to innovate. When we asked about making knowledge and skills effective and consequential in the real world, NTU scored only 4.65, despite a large number of engineers, while TIP scored 7.94.

We worried that TIP might have deteriorated to the level of 'vocational education', but only 4.41% claimed that this was the case. We also tested whether the NTU regarded practical skills and applications as 'impure' and 14.71% supported this, a large percentage for a school of technology. Even when a dilemma is worded so as to increase the university's chances of relegating TIP, it does so only by a small margin on one side of the dilemma. While only 11.76% of our sample placed university education in the reconciliation zone at top right, 35.29% placed TIP there. It is clear that using knowledge for practical ends does nothing to lessen profundity in this instance. TIP students pursue truth and seek to add to this.

DILEMMA 8 RATIONALITY, VERTICAL THINKING
AND VERIFICATION VS. LATERAL THINKING
AND INTER-DISCIPLINARY COMBINATIONS

Pursuing our determination to give NTU and the Scientific Method every chance to relegate TIP to an inferior status on at least one dimension, we gave respondents an opportunity to deem TIP 'unscientific' or falling short of university-approved disciplines. Did it come up to scratch in rationality, scepticism, empiricism and verification? It is most important that TIP does come up to scratch, because technopreneurship is supposed to combine disciplines at a high level of technological development. It cannot combine matrices of science usefully if it fails to uphold the rigours of the disciplines involved. We thought the university would far outscore TIP on this matter, but we were wrong. TIP needs to honour the sciences which it seeks to combine. A novel synthesis can only be as good as the disciplines from which it derives. We need to think 'vertically' and 'laterally' (see Edward de Bono).[7] Grid 5.8 shows the scores.

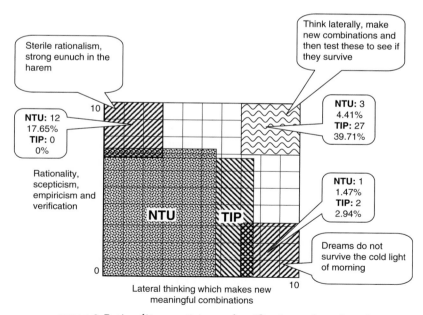

GRID 5.8 Rationality, scepticism and verification vs. lateral combinations

NTU covers 34.23 squares. TIP covers 52.91 or 59% higher ($R2 = 24.56\%$, $P<0.01$). NTU scored an impressive 7.29 but TIP scored only 0.41 beneath this or 6.88, a non-significant difference. It did so without any direct reference to research methodology or inducting students into a famous discipline. 17.65% of respondents agreed with the assertion that university courses made them into 'Strong Eunuchs in a Harem' – that is, clever but sterile – a phrase we borrowed from Edward de Bono. When it came to the second horn of this dilemma, the extent to which students are encouraged to think laterally and make new and valuable connections between disciplines, TIP beat NTU by a distance. The university scored 5.75 on lateral connectivity, while TIP scored 7.69. 39.71% of respondents scored TIP in the reconciliation zone, compared to 4.41% who put the university there. Clearly cross-disciplinary studies are somewhat neglected in the university at large, but it does succeed in teaching objective detachment, for which 48.53% placed it at 8, 9 or 10. Yet new combinations, not tried before, require the mastery of at least two disciplines cross-fertilizing one another. We had succeeded in establishing that TIP was more cross-disciplinary without losing respect for the disciplines themselves.

DILEMMA 9 HUMBLE QUESTIONING OF NATURE VS. BOLD INTERVENTION TO CHANGE THINGS

Still in pursuit of the university's redeeming values, we set out to discover if TIP lacked respect for the marvels of Nature and had descended into a mindless optimism about better mousetraps or similar trivialities. In the past, entrepreneurship has earned a reputation for bragging behaviours. 'History is bunk', Henry Ford is quoted as saying. Many became rich without attending the university and claimed to be self-made.

It is axiomatic that Nature reveals its laws only to those humble enough to serve a power greater than themselves, to seek reasons not yet their own, an order beyond their ken. The very word 'university' refers to the quest for universal truths vouchsafed only to the right questions. So we invited respondents to say whether the university or

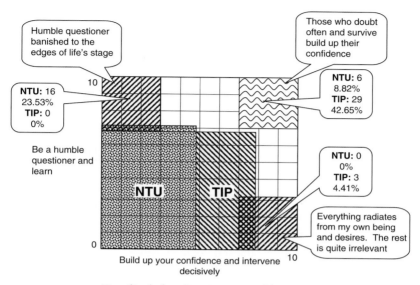

GRID 5.9 Humility before Creation vs. confidence to change it

TIP gave them more reason to marvel at the wonders of Nature and the universe. We expected the university to win easily. However, Grid 5.9 tells a different story.

NTU covers 33.94 squares. TIP covers 53.63, or 67% higher ($R2 = 26.67\%$, $P<0.01$). We were amazed to discover that the differences were minuscule. The university scored 7.08 and TIP 6.84, a non-significant difference of 0.24. Perhaps trying to innovate reminds you of existing Creation. But when it came to the self-confidence to intervene decisively, the university scored only 4.85 while TIP's score was 7.84. We wanted to test TIP for brash over-confidence. We tempted them by stating that 'Everything radiates from my own being', but only 4.41% fell for that nonsense. We took humility to excess by suggesting that university students had been 'banished to the edges of life's stage' and 23.53% believed this to be true: the Newtonian world of dead objects is indeed rather bleak. 42.65% of TIP students placed their work experience in the reconciliation zone, but only 8.82% found this to be true of university courses. Yet 61.76% of respondents had been sufficiently humbled by science teaching to score their courses 8, 9 and 10, another confirmation of the university's success by its own lights.

DILEMMA 10 ACHIEVEMENT BY PERFORMING
INDIVIDUALS VS. ACHIEVEMENT THROUGH
FULLY ENGAGED TEAMS

Here at last we found a measure by which the university outscored TIP decisively. We asked to what extent achievement relied upon the individual's personal performance and to what extent this was team-based and relational. Perhaps we dichotomized the question too much, since innovators need both personal conviction and the ability to rally teams around their projects. What we were looking for was achievement *through* others as opposed to *over* others.[8] Grid 5.10 shows the results.

NTU covers 35.51 squares. TIP covers 55.59, or 63% higher (R2 = 22.03%, P<0.01). TIP's score on individual performance was not low. 6.26 is respectable, but the university's was much higher, 7.75,

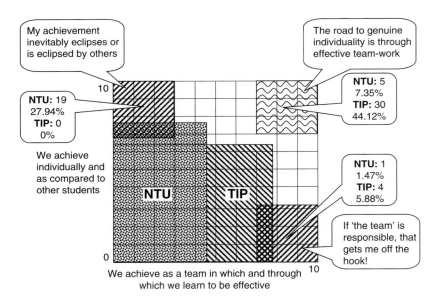

GRID 5.10 Individual vs. team achievement

which is higher by 1.49. However, the situation is reversed, with an additional margin, when we asked what the university contributed to team-work and interpersonal effectiveness. On this the university fell to 4.57 and TIP rose to 7.90, the largest gap in the whole survey. Team emphasis can be overdone, yet only 5.88% said that making the team responsible 'gets me off the hook'. But 27.94% complained that individual achievement meant 'eclipsing others' efforts'. A massive 44.12% reported TIP in the reconciliation zone, six times more than NTU.

DILEMMA II MERIT DEFINED BY AUTHORITIES
VS. SELF-DEFINED MERIT

We knew that when we touched on 'merit' there would be no compromise. Singapore is perhaps the world's most cleverly designed meritocracy. The only problem is that 'merit' is defined by the powers-that-be, who reward those who approximate to ideals espoused by the judges. What opens up a society to its full innovative potential is the right to define merit for yourself to see if others will agree with your definition.

As Grid 5.11 shows, the university scored 7.75 on merit being defined by authorities, while TIP scored 6.26. Note that they do not deny that authorities play a large part, they simply question that this is all of it. In contrast, the university falls to 4.57, less than half, when respondents are asked if they have any role in defining merit, while TIP scores 7.90 on this measure, even higher than the university's reliance on authority.

This was the university's largest lead over TIP on the vertical dimension. Even so on the 'squares test' NTU covered 34.34 squares and TIP 56.86, or 44% higher (R2 =13.76%, P<0.01). The university scored 7.75 on merit being defined by authorities, compared to TIP's 6.26. The proposition that in this university, 'To achieve you must agree with your superiors', was endorsed by 32.35%. This is a somewhat worrisome percentage. 13.24% of respondents agreed with the rebellious prompt 'We do as we please and authorities can lump it',

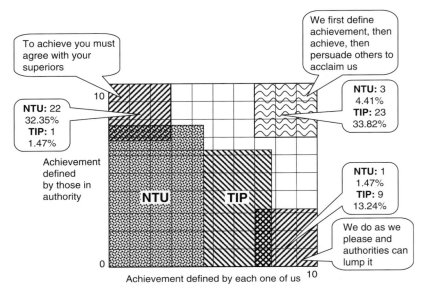

GRID 5.11 Merit defined by authorities vs. self

a somewhat juvenile attitude, yet excessive deference is still the greater problem!

The ideal, of course, is to define achievement yourself and get customers, allies and even authorities to agree with you. To that end 33.82% of the respondents said that TIP enabled reconciliation, while only 4.41% found this in their university courses. This was the smallest TIP reconciliation score recorded, the average being 41.98%. Perhaps it was not a fair question. Authorities take their time in approving innovative initiatives, praising them after they have succeeded and customers have been won over.

CONCLUSION AND FINAL PROOF OF SUCCESS

We have looked at the scores for the eleven dilemmas and found that TIP scores considerably better on all lateral dimensions, while not being below NTU on the traditional, vertical dimensions by any significant margin, so that TIP may be said to uphold the university standards. However, the most remarkable finding is that nearly 42% of all

TIP students scored their pedagogy in the reconciliation zone, eight times more than the same students scored their undergraduate courses at NTU. This unique capacity to integrate contrasting educational processes would seem to be TIP's greatest virtue. Yet there remains one nagging question. The purpose of this programme was not primarily to be well assessed by those who participated in it, encouraging although this is. The programme is not an end in itself but a means to making its members more innovative and entrepreneurial. Is there any evidence that they became so? There is.

By January 2008 154 students had started 46 business ventures, employing about 75 of their number. This had happened despite the fact that:

(a) Many had not joined the programme to become entrepreneurs.
(b) Twenty or more had gone on to get their MSc degree of which this programme was a module.
(c) Most are in debt when they graduate.
(d) The course advises them to get experience in their selected area of innovation before launching their own ventures.
(e) They have an average of only two to three years to launch such a venture.

We contend that forty-six surviving start-ups is a very remarkable result. If only 10% of these eventually prosper they will have repaid the cost of the course several times over.

6 Results of the Mandarin-speaking programme

Instructing Chinese students from the PRC in Mandarin turned out to be a very different experience from instructing Singaporeans and others in English. Professor Tan experienced them both since he is bilingual, a rare advantage in modern Singapore, where many elite Singaporeans have lost their native tongue. Professor Clayton Christiansen, this author and several other faculty members had their presentations translated into Mandarin by Tan Teng-Kee, a somewhat exhausting process for him. Both programmes included the 'ecosystem' described in Chapter 2 with visits to the USA and China. The two classes met and mingled.

Those teaching both classes quickly noticed some differences. Here is a summary of our earlier impressions.

> The Chinese students had few, if any, of the inhibitions against showing off and attracting attention to themselves that characterized the Singaporean class. The Chinese were more extravagant and playful, and preferred to talk rather than listen.
>
> They took much longer to achieve membership of a coherent team. Both we and the Chinese themselves attributed this to the 'one child per family' policy of the PRC. This one child has two parents, four grandparents, usually no siblings and is the centre of adult attention. They are treated like 'Little Emperors or Empresses'. They lack interaction with peers.
>
> Chinese students were much more likely to have studied 'soft' subjects, the liberal arts, humanities and social sciences. These have been relatively neglected in Singapore in favour of teaching business, science and engineering.
>
> The programme appears to have attracted members of the Chinese elite, including media celebrities and the children of the

ruling class. The forty available places are over-subscribed at US$40,000 a head, more than most of the Singaporean candidates can afford, despite the per capita income in Singapore being five times higher than that in the PRC. Chinese participants are more overtly emotional, more diverse, more visionary and imaginative, more philosophic and poetic and have a Mandarin vocabulary much larger than the English vocabulary used by most Singaporeans.

On the other hand, Chinese students are noticeably less rigorous, less systematic, less disciplined, less focused and less 'left-brain dominant' than Singaporeans. They are less in awe of hard science and less respectful of Anglo-American empiricism. They are less objective and detached. The Chinese students appear to have more influence within their cultures. Invited to study and understand innovative feats of Chinese enterprise, they located the persons concerned, brought them into class and even had them coach team projects.

They are more ambitious in their use of prototypes, using holographic images and three-dimensional models.

They are less likely to ask permission before surprising you and appear far more interested in the long-term effects of their work.

They are more likely to grasp that the model of innovation used in this programme has profound impacts beyond the class, beyond economics and wealth creation, and constitutes a new morality for living. They asked this author to sign his handouts as keepsakes. His work has special resonance for Chinese culture.

The role of the teacher seems more honoured in China and those they admire are showered with gifts and personal notes of thanks. The photographing of students posing with their teacher individually and severally takes up to an hour!

The view of the teacher is much more diffuse and inclusive – guide, philosopher, friend, coach and 'father'. They are more likely to try and keep in touch electronically, despite language barriers.

> Age is thought to confer wisdom and older teachers are asked for advice in general on topics not covered in the course.
>
> Pride in what China has accomplished in the last thirty years is palpable and there is visible delight in its re-telling.

Sadly, what we lack with the Mandarin class is evidence of the number of start-ups which students are responsible for. This is because the course was barely a year old when our evaluation was made and too little time had elapsed. Nevertheless, we worry that studying innovation abroad in Singapore and the USA may be too much of a fashion statement for the sons and daughters of the Chinese elite. Elites have not contributed much to entrepreneurship historically, although the Chinese case may be exceptional.

Curiously, the Mandarin class rarely complains about meeting the $40,000 course fees, while the English-speaking Singaporeans seem to find this much harder. The suspicion is that the Chinese class is drawn from top-earning members of the Chinese elite and that the Singaporeans are closer to the marginal/migrant middle-class profile of entrepreneurs in general. Prof. Tan commented:

> I find the Chinese students more exciting and inspiring to teach. They never cease to amaze me. That said, I find the Singaporeans 'hungrier' and better equipped to confront world-class competition. They seem to know better what they are up against and how hard it is going to be.

COMPARATIVE RESULTS

I shall not work through all eleven dilemmas, as I did in Chapter 5, since the overall pattern becomes clear after five or six. Generally speaking NTU, as a preparation for the TIP course, outscores the average of the Chinese universities, but those universities are far less skewed towards traditional Western values and are better balanced between our dual objectives, realism and idealism. Chinese university pedagogy strays less often into the 'pathology zones' at the top left and bottom right of our grids.

DILEMMA I INTELLECTUAL ORDERING VS. EMOTIONAL EXPERIENCE

Grid 6.1 shows the results for Dilemma 1 on intellectual mastery vs. experience and emotion. We may recall that NTU closely matched TIP on the issue of intellectuality, but Chinese universities rate themselves significantly below TIP and below the ratings Singaporeans gave NTU.

Chinese universities score themselves 5.8 on intellectuality compared with TIP's 7.3 and they rate their remembered courses 4.6 on experience compared to TIP's 7.5, a gap of almost three points. On experience there is no significant difference between NTU's undergraduate courses and those of Chinese universities: both score below 5. Lecturing appears to be the preferred mode.

But Chinese universities are less biased towards traditional values and fewer of their students stray into the 'pathology zone' at top left. Only 7.94% of Chinese students describe the degree of intellectuality as 'remote, abstract, ivory tower, feelings play no part', but fully 16.18% of NTU students agreed with this description in Chapter 5, over twice as many. Of Chinese students taking the TIP

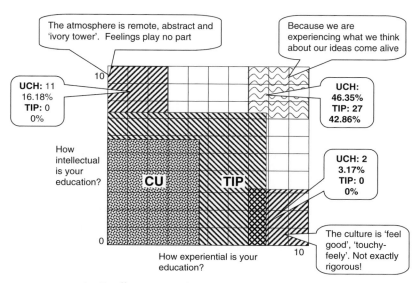

GRID 6.1 Intellect vs. experience

programme, 42.86% reached the reconciliation zone, compared with 44.12% of Singaporean students. However, Chinese students show larger overall gains taking their undergraduate pedagogy as a base.

It would seem that Chinese undergraduate education lacks the intellectual rigour of the equivalent courses at NTU, but that fewer Chinese students feel alienated and emotionally bereft.

DILEMMA 2 ABSORBING INFORMATION TOP-DOWN VS. THINKING AND DOING FROM BOTTOM-UP

Chinese education as a whole has long been accused of relying too much on learning by rote. Students over the centuries have been required to memorize passages from classic texts and recite these. We were on the look-out for any signs that this might still be true, in which case rote learning would show up in high levels of absorption and minimal levels of doing anything with that knowledge, which is necessary for innovation.

As anticipated, Grid 6.2 shows that learning by thinking and doing was low in Chinese universities, 4.5 out of 10, but then it was

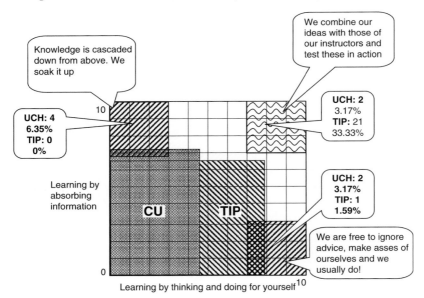

GRID 6.2 Absorbing information vs. thinking and doing

not much better among Singaporean respondents, 4.6 out of 10. The difference is not statistically significant. Only 3.17% of Chinese students reached the reconciliation zone through undergraduate courses, very slightly better than the 2.94% reported among the Singaporean English-speaking students, but not significant either.

However, Chinese students responded well to the TIP course with a hefty 33.33% reaching the reconciliation zone, almost identical to the Singaporeans at 32.35%. Once again the Singaporeans complained more of the unequal emphasis on absorbing information. Nearly 30% (29.41%) agreed with the statement 'Knowledge is cascaded down from above. We soak it up', compared to only 6.35% of Chinese students making this complaint. Neither culture reported that they were free to ignore advice and make asses of themselves to any substantial degree. TIP increased those achieving reconciliation by a factor of ten in both programmes.

DILEMMA 3 COMPETING ON THE LEVEL PLAYING FIELD VS. COOPERATING IN AN EXTENDED FAMILY

The 'Level Playing Field' is very much an American metaphor and we would therefore expect NTU education to be pulled in that direction. We might expect the metaphor to be weaker in China. In contrast, metaphors having to do with the family would be strong in both cultures.

As expected, Grid 6.3 shows that the Chinese scored their undergraduate education at their universities slightly lower, at 6.05 on the level-playing-field vertical axis, compared with 6.91 for estimates of NTU in Chapter 5.

Only 33.33% of Chinese students reached the reconciliation zone as a result of the TIP class, compared with 44.12% of the Singaporean students reported in Chapter 5, although the latter started from a significantly lower base-line. But Chinese students were again less likely to show signs of alienation. Only 14.29% complained that it was 'every person for himself' at their universities. This was said by 22.06% of students from NTU undergraduate courses. Also, Chinese

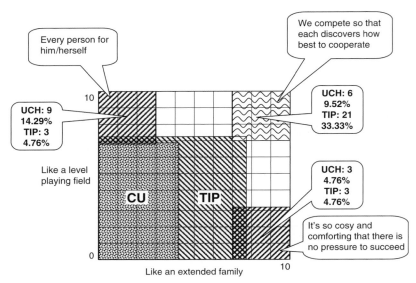

GRID 6.3 The level playing field vs. the extended family

universities were more likely to have reached the reconciliation zone in their undergraduate classes. 9.52% said this had been achieved compared with 2.94% of NTU students, although the numbers in both cases are very small compared to TIP, which succeeded in promoting a 'family atmosphere' in both Singaporean and Chinese programmes. As usual very few TIP students fell into the two pathology zones of excessive cosiness or ruthless competition.

DILEMMA 4 SERIOUS HARD WORK VS. PLAYFUL ENJOYMENT

Playing, but for serious ends, is one of the most salient characteristics of learning to innovate. We wondered whether China might be serious to the point of being 'grim and strenuous' like undergraduate classes at NTU and indeed, as shown in Grid 6.4, 20.63% (more than one-fifth) reported this to be the case. But we may recall from Chapter 5 that 22.06% of Singaporeans reported this. No one at either Chinese universities or NTU reported their courses to be too playful! On this dimension 31.73% of the Mandarin class found their way into the

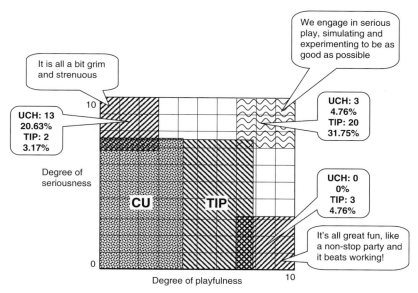

GRID 6.4 Seriousness vs. playfulness

reconciliation zone, well short of the Singaporean TIP's 50% reported in the last chapter.

Clearly the whole concept of being playful by using simulations, rehearsing, prototypes and low-cost failures remains alien to universities in general. They take themselves far too seriously for such 'foolishness'. To fail in the early stages of high aspiration does not find a place in these rather solemn pedagogies. Students are to be correct as a condition of preferment without any slip-ups. The impression of universities in general as discouraging innovation is strengthened by these results.

DILEMMA 5 CAREER CONTINUITY AND MASTERING CHOSEN PATHS VS. TRANSFORMATION OF YOURSELF AND RE-INVENTION

We thought that the amazingly rapid development of the Chinese economy[1] might have made them keener to undergo transformation.[2] Perhaps so, but this urge does not seem to have reached their universities.

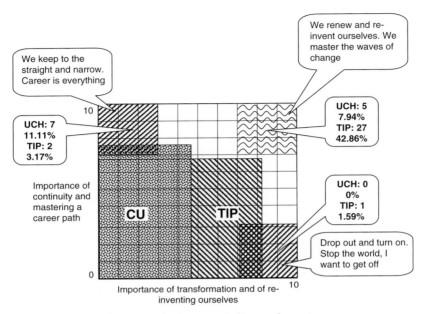

GRID 6.5 Career continuity vs. periodic transformation

Chinese universities scored only 5 out of 10 on transformation, better than NTU at 4.6, but not much better. However, this does seem to have helped 42.86% of the Mandarin-speaking programme to reach their reconciliation zone close behind the Singaporean class at 47.06%.

Once again Grid 6.5 shows the TIP Mandarin class outscoring Chinese universities on both dimensions, career mastery *and* transformation/re-invention, despite the scant attention given to career paths in the TIP course. And again the Mandarin class was better balanced with only 11.11% reporting 'We keep to the straight and narrow. Career is everything', while 25% of the English-speaking class subscribed to this statement. The Chinese students also avoided the pitfall into which 10.29% of the English-speaking TIP students fell at bottom right, 'Drop out and turn on. Stop the world, I want to get off.' Clearly a class can be *too* turbulent, but not this Mandarin class, where only 1.59% experienced this dizziness.

DILEMMA 6 HARD OBJECTIVITY VS. NEGATIVE
FEEDBACK AMID RAPPORT

We argued that there were two different kinds of toughness required, the first by scientists observing objectively and the second by innovators confronting negative feedback. Might the Chinese Mandarin programme score better on either of these? We believed that innovative persons had to have both these values.

Grid 6.6 shows that, on this particular dimension, 41.27% of the Mandarin class placed themselves in the reconciliation zone, compared to 48.3% of the English-speaking Singaporean class, but once again Chinese students improved markedly from a lower base. TIP again outscored Chinese universities on the traditional dimension as well as the 'progressive' one. But fewer Chinese students found objectivity in undergraduate studies too 'painful' to report – 12.70% compared to 20.59%. A negligible number of students used their mutual rapport to hide disagreeable truths from each other.

What might account for the English-speaking class achieving slightly better results? One obvious reason is that they rated their

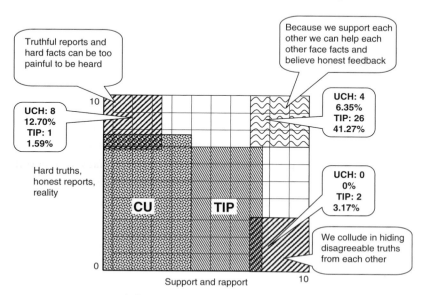

GRID 6.6 Hard objectivity vs. negative feedback amid rapport

undergraduate classes higher, so that they improved from a higher base-line. Another possible reason was that the English-speaking faculty had to have their presentations translated which reduces their length by 50% even if nothing is lost in the translation. It is difficult to assemble a Mandarin-speaking faculty, although Tan Teng-Kee is common to both programmes. Finally, the values being measured are household words in the West but may be less familiar to Chinese speakers, who might be slower to recognize their presence and applaud this.

I shall not go into details over the remaining five dilemmas. Suffice it here to say that the results are remarkably consistent. It seems to matter less which particular values are chosen than whether the respondent polarizes, compromises or reconciles these. Roughly the same level of reconciliation is achieved whichever pair of values is measured, a phenomenon which suggests that whether or not we fuse values may matter more than what those values are. What the programmes appear to have imparted to between 20% and 50% of their participants is the capacity to reconcile contrasting values in a novel synthesis. Since all the values are variants on Realism/Idealism we may be measuring the capacity to resolve these over and over again in slightly different ways.

There comes a point where value contrasts are handled in such a way that their boundaries collapse, the ideal becomes the real, the experience becomes intellectualized, top-down information is absorbed and thrust back into the culture bottom-up, the level playing field gains the benefits of having coaches and cheering sections on the sidelines, and the play becomes serious as the day of the product launch approaches. All these contrasts fuse because novel synthesis is a characteristic of innovation itself.

But this is not to say that the specific questions are unimportant. Just how important is shown by an error we made in using Dilemma 11 with our Chinese sample. This question contrasts 'Merit as defined by authorities' with 'Merit as defined by yourself'. We were at first dismayed by the poor reconciliation numbers on this dimension scored by our Chinese respondents, only 14.29%, dragging their average down. This compared to 33.82% by the Singaporean respondents.

Then we saw why. We were asking the Chinese respondents whether they could reconcile self-defined merit learned in Singapore with what Chinese authorities wanted of them. Those were not Singaporean authorities who had sponsored and subsidized the TIP programme and wanted it to succeed. They were Chinese authorities, who knew little or nothing about this unauthorized experiment. Obviously, the Chinese students would have a far harder time convincing their authorities about the virtues learnt in a foreign country. We had failed to ask a comparable question because the definition of 'authority' was at great variance in the two cases.

But in a sense the error was fortunate because it shows that respondents were paying careful attention to the questions and would report disappointing results accurately. Although the question was the last to be answered a 'response set' had not become habitual.

COMPARISON OF ALL ELEVEN DILEMMAS

We are now in a position to contrast Chinese university undergraduate programmes with Chinese TIP across both traditional values on the vertical axes and 'progressive' values on the horizontal axes. Progressive values do not amount to innovation. What renders people innovative is reconciling the two sets of values.

Here we see that TIP actually outscored Chinese universities on traditional values, although it was not consciously emphasizing these. The exception is Dilemma 11 whose errors on our part have been explained. This provides the strongest evidence that traditional values actually support innovative pedagogy when properly taught. On eight dilemmas out of eleven TIP outscores Chinese universities by small but significant margins. These were values it took for granted since they were so dominant at NUT. On another two values TIP leads, but not significantly.

In the history of Chinese science and discovery, there are many outstanding inventions, some of which precede the West by a century or more. However, a number of these were lost sight of when one dynasty replaced another.[3] The problem may lie in a reluctance to codify knowledge so that it is easily passed on to succeeding generations. Perhaps we are seeing some residues of this here. It seems that codified, traditional values imported from the West remain stronger in Singapore, even where undergraduate programmes are compared.

When we turn to the 'progressive' values on the horizontal axes, then the extent to which the TIP Mandarin programme outstripped the undergraduate experience at Chinese universities becomes dramatically clear.

There was an especially large gain in the 'learning through teamwork' measure (Dilemma 10). We argued earlier that the Chinese from one-child families had little practice with peer-group interaction. There is almost as large a gain on Dilemma 9, the realization that 'Nature can be altered to change destinies boldly'. Several of these gains are between 20% and 30%. Fewer Chinese students reached the reconciliation zone, 36.0% on average, compared with 41.8% in the English-language programme. Yet if we remove the 'unfair' Dilemma 11, this brings the Chinese average up to 38.17% and the difference is barely significant.

We may conclude that this pedagogy joins West with East, America and the UK (where Tan Teng-Kee was trained) with the Chinese culture in which he was raised and NTU from which he graduated. Innovation is not simply vital to affluent economies and those now catching up, but appears to mediate between nations and cultures using their diversity to create wealth. Ideas which bridge cultures seem to be innovative by definition. They create 'remote associations', the key to creativity.

7 Reconciling values: a helical model of innovative processes

Thus far we have measured the innovative process using square grids, but these fail to reveal how values are actually synthesized or the process by which participants learn to do this. We have seen that you need not just intellect or experience, but both, intellectualized or codified experience. You need not just to absorb top-down instruction but to initiate bottom-up thoughts and actions, or commitments to some of what you have absorbed. Instead of just competing on a metaphorical 'level playing field', you need the cooperation of colleagues and an extended 'family' that coach and critique your play.

Your product is unlikely to be right first time, so you need many rehearsals before friendly, yet critical, audiences. You need to play with your ideas in a safe place, where failings are understood, but all this is for a very serious purpose, success in the open market for which you must prepare yourself. This helps summarize earlier discussions, but how can these processes be structured in a consistent way? Can we model reconciled values?

VALUE SYSTEMS ARE CIRCULAR AND CYBERNETIC
It has been recognized for some time that values are systems. They are not isolated objects and no sense can be made if they are treated as if they were. Values are not things but *differences*.[1] Hence top-down is different from bottom-up, cooperating is different from competing and so on. If you doubt this try defining one end of such a continuum without defining the contrasting end. The meaning lies in the difference or contrast. To be playful is not to be serious and vice versa. These values are not only circular but cybernetic. The word comes from the Greek *kybernetes* meaning 'helmsman'. We use values to steer ourselves to be now more cooperative, now more competitive,

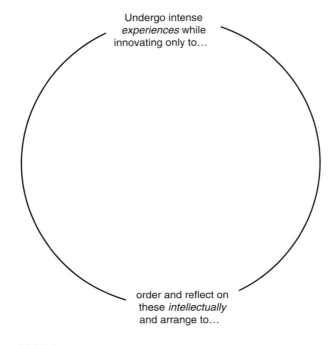

Undergo intense *experiences* while innovating only to…

order and reflect on these *intellectually* and arrange to…

CIRCLE I

now more playful, now more serious. This resembles a captain steering his ship when winds and tides are blowing it off course. For example, we have intense experiences when innovating, which we then order intellectually (see Circle 1).

Some of these experiences will be more valuable and illuminating than others and we will use our intellects to organize those experiences coherently. What we have here is a *learning loop* corrected by our own experiences, so that we steer towards preferred outcomes. From another of our paired values we might learn too (see Circle 2).

As this system resolves we are better able to attend the lectures, or expose ourselves to the instruction imparted by teachers that we deem most relevant to our interests. The information received top-down and initiatives pushed from the bottom up become ever more closely aligned and reconciled. Once again we are steering

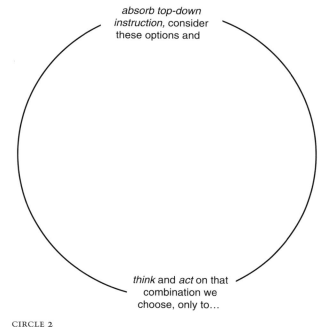

absorb top-down instruction, consider these options and

think and *act* on that combination we choose, only to…

CIRCLE 2

cybernetically and learning from feedback. Or consider our third pair of values: competing / cooperating. We need to maintain this clear difference, but we also need to move from one to the other on a continuum, first competing then cooperating to help that competing. Circle 3 shows how we accomplish this.

Here is yet another revolving system. In this case friends and 'family' help us examine the feedback from the level playing field and coach us into extensive improvement. We are egged on by coaching and by our cheering section. Everyone concerned is learning better to cooperate so as to compete more effectively. The two contrasting values are synergistic. They develop as one.

Finally, consider our fourth pair: playfulness / seriousness. Once again we need both and we need them to be very different, very playful and extremely serious. They must be both differentiated and integrated, a theme running through all life sciences. Circle 4 shows how we play now to be serious later and continue to play until completely

compete on a level playing field, but we are immeasurably helped

by the *cooperation* of an *extended family* of critical supporters who help us...

CIRCLE 3

satisfied and ready for the very serious business of launching a new product. The play steers and guides us towards serious ends.

All four of these value systems are self-regulating, self-organizing and self-correcting. The particular mix of play and seriousness, cooperating and competing must be varied over time and over shifting circumstances. What is clear, however, is that all four differences need to be encompassed in any innovative synthesis.

FROM CIRCLES TO HELICES

But circles are not quite enough to do justice to the innovative process. It is quite possible to go round and round and finish where you started like a dog chasing his own tail. Indeed it may be worse. It is possible for the values discussed here to form a vicious circle. Those who have enjoyed intense experiences may be anti-intellectual, while the cerebral may scorn all experience. Students in a classroom may be so

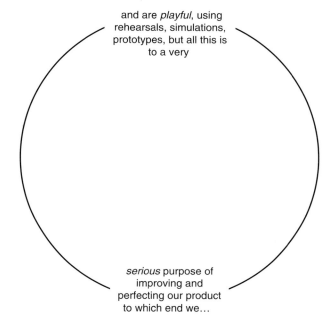

CIRCLE 4

playful and rowdy that no serious education occurs, or so grim and serious that the joy of learning is lost.

It is quite possible for the level of competing to get out of hand. Students have been known to tear pages out of library books so that only they can benefit from reading them and they will steal a march on rivals. In such cases cooperation among students has been expunged. Alternatively students can become complicit in not competing and not showing up the less able among them. But this collusion prevents us learning how we might improve from mistakes and failings. The vicious circle runs as shown in Circle 5.

Notice that both virtuous and vicious circles are self-perpetuating. Hiding from each other the fact that we may be failing in our learning harms our competitiveness, which provides even stronger temptation to hide this truth. The vicious circle is also steered in cybernetic feedback, but in this case it functions to lower our anxiety about incipient disaster by hiding the facts from us.

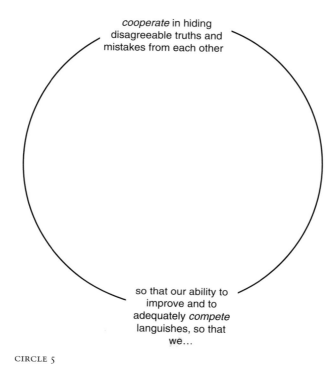

CIRCLE 5

Playfulness/seriousness can form a vicious circle as can all our eleven value pairs. We can be too playful or play too long, as is shown in Circle 6.

As the time to launch the product approaches we linger within the adult playpen we have created and indefinitely postpone the cold shock of reality. Of course, the vicious circle can be written with the other value, seriousness, too dominant. In this case we take the encounter with the market so seriously and are so grimly realistic about this that we never learn to play and so never prepare ourselves properly, never dare to make mistakes and so cannot improve.

One important characteristic of genuine learning is that values not only correct each other, so that the helmsman balances the ship and keeps on course, but the values actually enhance each other. It is because the experiences are so intense and so profound that intellectual lessons are the more illuminating and you know where to steer to

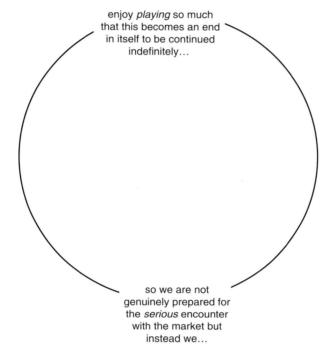

enjoy *playing* so much that this becomes an end in itself to be continued indefinitely…

so we are not genuinely prepared for the *serious* encounter with the market but instead we…

CIRCLE 6

realize more of these. It is because the play was so enjoyable and hence so prolonged that you are now ready for the serious business of the product launch, the success of which enables you to play again. It is because your extended family supported yet critiqued you so thoroughly that you can now defeat the competition and learn even more from your coaches.

HELICAL MODELS OF THE INNOVATIVE PROCESS

One way to portray a virtuous circle is by means of a helix spiralling upwards, while a vicious circle would be a helix spiralling downwards. Every revolution of the upward spiral represents a higher level of intellectuality and experience, absorption from top down and thinking / doing from bottom up, cooperating and competing. Playfulness and seriousness ascend sequentially yet together, the first preparing the ground for the second.

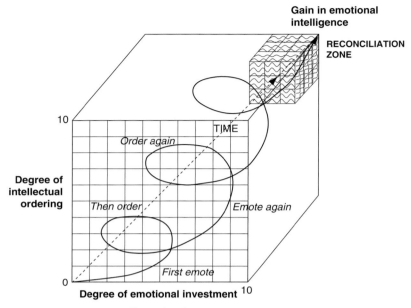

DILEMMA I Intellectual ordering vs. emotional experience

In order to depict this properly we need to extend the square or grid we have been using. It is not wrong, but nor is it enough. Instead we will create a cube and portray the upward spiral of the learning process as a helix within that cube. This is done below to our first dilemma of intellectual ordering vs. emotional experience (Dilemma 1).

Note that this helix is anti-clockwise. Learners first invest themselves emotionally in a new venture which represents their aspirations, but they must order intelligently the results of this experience so that the spiral moves back towards the vertical axis as they make sense of that investment. Only then can they emote again and organize again. Note that this happens over time and that the arrow of time moves from the near bottom-left-hand corner of our cube to the far top-right-hand corner, as the helix spirals around it. The reconciliation zone is now at the far top-right-hand corner, where the helix culminates. Those reaching this, approximately 40 per cent of the TIP class, have achieved higher emotional intelligence, through the

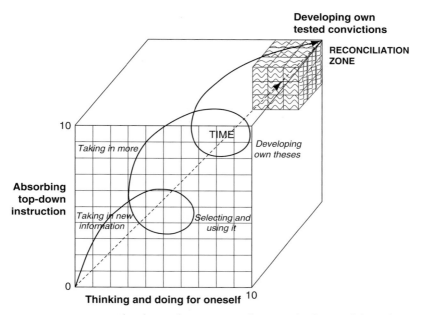

DILEMMA 2 Absorbing information top-down vs. thinking and doing from bottom-up

progressive integration of emotional experience with intellectual ordering.

There is no inherent reason why experience should precede intellectual ordering, although we suspect it does so now more commonly than it did in the past. Much depends on the participants' learning style.[2] Some will seize on intellectual constructs because these make sense of remembered experiences, but most, we think, will plunge in at the deep end, experience first and then try to order that experience. It is not always a useful exercise to argue about where a circle starts.

Our second dilemma was mediating top-down instruction and bottom-up initiatives which had been selected from the broad array of this instruction. The information has to come from somewhere and paying careful attention to lessons is probably essential to learning, but so is thinking, doing and testing your own convictions. This process is illustrated in Dilemma 2.

Here we believe that a clockwise helix makes more sense. The learner needs a considerable amount of information initially, if he/she is to choose the best possible combinations to think with and to enact. Yet again, there are different learning styles. One reason that innovators and entrepreneurs are often drop-outs and late developers is that they pay very selective attention to instruction and regurgitate this insufficiently to please their mentors.

Nevertheless, the first step must be to take in information – only then can you select what you use as the helix winds to the right. You commit yourself to the combination you have wrought and seek still more information to test this proposition. The aim is to reach the reconciliation zone at top far right where innovators develop their own tested convictions. This is what a doctoral thesis was originally supposed to mean, the testing via research of original thought, although those who wish to make a career for themselves at particular institutions might be wise to test the ideas of their supervisor. New theories are rarely welcome, especially from younger people.

Most teachers are more adept at noticing that their instructions have been heeded than at evaluating the originality of students. Indeed with a ratio of thirty plus students to each teacher, bringing out the originality of the former would be a daunting task and is rarely attempted. This is why the ratio of students to helpers is almost 1 to 1 in the TIP course and as much as 1 to 2 in the Cambridge entrepreneurial class run by Professor Shai Vyakarnam.[3] If we do not elicit 'thinking and doing for oneself', it cannot develop, as most university classes show.

Our third pair of innovative values was competing vs. cooperating. In this instance the family-style primary group within the programme participants, including the small group or team structure, helped to prepare members of the class for the savage and competitive world 'out there'. However, it would be naïve to pretend that even within the class participants do not compete. Competition is vital to learning about oneself, what one does well and less well. This is all part of the self-knowledge crucial to innovation (see Dilemma 3).

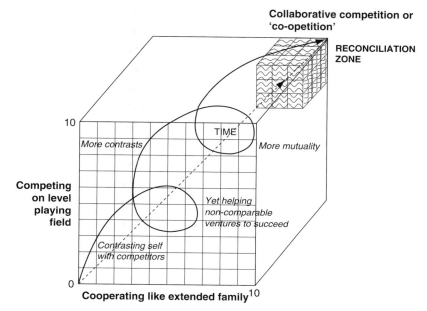

DILEMMA 3 Competing on the level playing field vs. cooperating in an extended family

When students first enter the course and do not know each other well they compete, anxiously contrasting their abilities with those of their companions and learning how they compare and where strengths and weaknesses lie. This is an important lesson and cannot be avoided. A future entrepreneur must choose his/her companions to compensate for any weakness.

However, as the course progresses it becomes increasingly clear that the ventures chosen are non-comparable, with no one's success detracting from that of anyone else, since aims are so diverse. Each person can help companies to success without dimming their own lustre, so unique are the aspirations. Yet the process of competing and contrasting never goes away either. Other persons will be more articulate, have a more convincing prototype or business plan, will convince more thoroughly, visiting venture capitalists. The most outstanding features of different ventures are likely to be emulated. The process culminates in the collaborative competition of 'co-opetition',

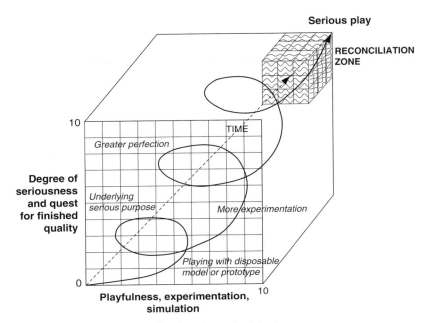

DILEMMA 4 Serious hard work vs. playful enjoyment

as it has been called, with most competitive features of people's ventures becoming advantages for others to cooperate around. In many ways we compete at cooperating more effectively. The better the internal cooperation, the better is the external competition.

Our fourth contrast or value difference was high degrees of seriousness vs. high degrees of playfulness. Playfulness includes experimentation, simulation, repeated rehearsals and the extensive use of prototypes and models. The idea is to make many inexpensive mistakes and learn from this. Seriousness is justified by the very real prospect of catastrophic failure and losing the venture into which you have poured your heart and your treasure. The situation is epitomized in the diagram for Dilemma 4.

We are more confident of the anti-clockwise helix in this case because playfulness precedes seriousness. When you are still highly uncertain and tentative you play. As you become more certain of your innovation and the crucial market-test draws near, things become serious. By then you must have everything looking right. However, that does not mean you stop playing. When NASA launches a spacecraft a computer simulation runs twenty to thirty seconds ahead of the launch. If a snag is spotted the launch can be aborted saving hundreds of millions of dollars.[4] A computerized spread-sheet is used to simulate the take-over of another company – as the negotiators bargain the spread-sheet spells out the consequences of different moves.[5] But in all cases 'play' precedes serious decisions with momentous consequences and perfection is approximated as far as possible as the result of simulated trials. This process has been called 'serious play'.[6]

Our fifth value difference was the continuity of career path vs. the transforming of the industry and re-invention of yourself. There can be no denying that knowledge is organized into disciplines and career paths to try to keep specialists within these disciplines. Crossing boundaries can be unpopular. Who do you think you are? Moreover the mastery of a career may be essential to understanding what is happening at the frontiers of knowledge. Information is largely cumulative and if you are not of that discipline you may not grasp it. And the evidence that major breakthroughs of transformative impact occur *between* disciplines is undeniable.[7] The situation is laid out in the diagram for Dilemma 5.

Anyone into sound engineering would be wise to know music. If lithography is the clue to making smaller chips you had better know that field. If the human genome is going to revolutionize medical diagnostics then the bridge between biology and medicine is the key to success. Genetics will be the next dominant language.[8] If we examine this helix we see that single career paths can join into new specialities and industries, which in turn create whole new fields of endeavour. The idea is to cross-fertilize two or more continuities to get specialities to break into one another's fields and see the world anew. This time the helix is clockwise since some kind of continuing cumulative discipline is essential before transformation can occur.

Dilemma 6 considers two disciplined ways of confronting uncomfortable truths. Learners are taught to be objective and

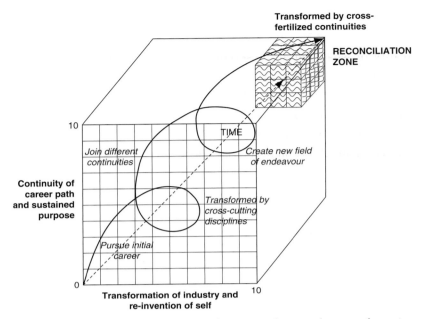

DILEMMA 5 Career continuity and mastering chosen path vs. transformation of yourself and re-invention

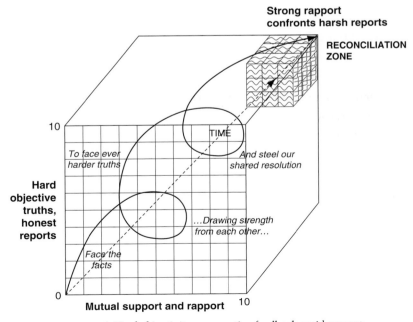

DILEMMA 6 Hard objectivity vs. negative feedback amid rapport

dispassionate. The world is what it is, not something they have ardently wished for. It is necessary to detach your person from the reality of what you are observing. Strong desires may distort your perception.

But there is quite another way of steeling yourself to truth and that is by relying on the critical acumen of trusted friends and colleagues. A new product is very likely to fail, despite yearnings for it to succeed, and relying on negative feedback from persons you know are trying to help you is a powerful prod towards improving your product while there is still time. Better by far to face doubting colleagues than consumers refusing to buy. Your critic can save you in the nick of time.

We see objectivity as important but not sufficient. It tends to dampen passion. The passive observer is not the origin of anything new. You need the strength of your colleagues, their sceptical affection and support as the helix moves right, so that you can face ever harder truths if necessary. The steely resolution will be shared only when doubts are laid to rest and strong rapport grapples with tough reports.[9]

Entrepreneurship and innovation have always suffered for their lack of 'purity' and for being applied sciences sullied by commerce. This introduces us to another value dichotomy, the pursuit of pure and profound knowledge for its own sake, contrasted with knowledge directed towards practical use (see Dilemma 7). The first tends to be respectable and praiseworthy. Nature has her own logics, not necessarily our own. The second tends to be tinged with vulgarity for having an ulterior purpose.

But, of course, practical knowledge is based on knowledge of nature. Once we know nature's secrets we can harness them. That's why the helix first moves towards the vertical axis in search of profound knowledge and only then exploits its practicalities. But we are very unwise to scorn practical knowledge. In many instances it is quicker to make mistakes and correct these through successive approximations than to theorize intensively and apply that knowledge later. Many corporations now lead universities in key fields of endeavour, and pragmatic approaches to knowledge are invaluable. Nature itself, through evolution, is the product of successive trials with the

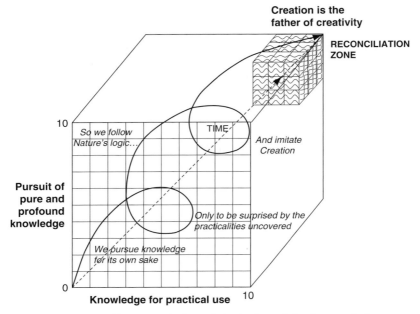

DILEMMA 7 Pure quest for knowledge vs. knowledge for practical use

creatures best adapted to their environments surviving. If we look at the reconciliation zone we see that Creation is the father of creativity. It abounds with brilliant examples of strategic survival, which inspire us all.

Our eighth dilemma contrasts vertical thinking with its means–ends rationalism, empiricism and verification with lateral thinking that makes meaningful combinations out of these lines of thought.[10] Universities teach us how what we have discovered can be verified and codified. They only rarely teach us the logic of discovery itself (see Dilemma 8).

Since academia is already full of silos of information enclosed within disciplinary boundaries, we encouraged participants in TIP to think laterally and start joining these bodies of knowledge in search of innovative combinations. This is why the anti-clockwise helix moves first to the right to make lateral connections. Yet all these new connections need to be passed from the right- to the left-brain hemisphere

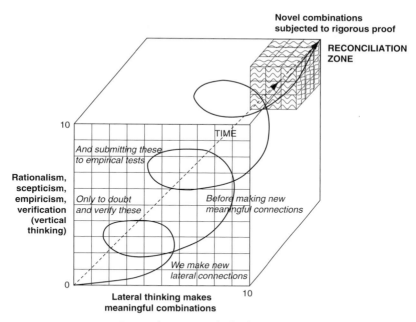

DILEMMA 8 Rationality, vertical thinking and verification vs. lateral thinking and inter-disciplinary combinations

to be verified and codified on the left of our diagram. Our belief that we have made exciting new connections needs to be tested and systematically doubted using customary disciplines. Our novel combinations must be submitted to rigorous proof in the reconciliation zone (top right).

In Dilemma 9 we contrast 'Asking humble questions of Nature' with 'Intervening boldly to change things'. These are two very different mind-sets. Moreover, the idea that our minds are just retinal mirrors, reflecting God-given realities 'out there', is almost certainly false. There is increasing evidence that what we call Nature is in fact the interaction between our nervous systems, our tools of measurement and the physical and biological universe. We 'see' selectively what our tools were evolved to uncover.

For all such reasons our human shadow looms over our fields of inquiry. Despite denials we help to shape what we discover. Sight,

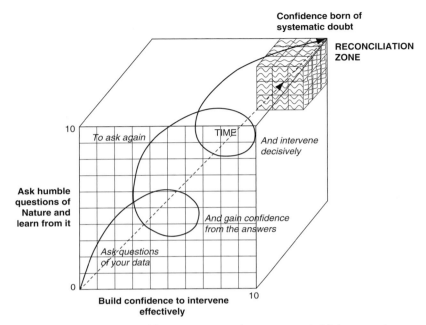

Confidence born of
systematic doubt

RECONCILIATION
ZONE

10

To ask again

TIME

And intervene
decisively

Ask humble
questions of
Nature and
learn from it

And gain confidence
from the answers

Ask questions
of your data

0

10

Build confidence to intervene
effectively

DILEMMA 9 Humble questioning of Nature vs. bold intervention to change things

sound, colour, shape are all inside ourselves, not simply a quality of what we are investigating. This helix goes clockwise because it is wise to know Nature as well as possible before hazarding an intervention. We can only get answers if we ask the right questions. The humility of our questions comes from systematic doubt. We keep asking if we are wrong, but in the end comes a confidence born of the fact that we have survived doubt repeatedly and have had our hypotheses confirmed. Hence in the reconciliation zone at top right is 'Confidence born of systematic doubt'. We have verified so often that we have become certain.

Our tenth contrasting pair of values is achieving and excelling as individuals compared to others vs. achieving and excelling with and through a team. If we are serious about innovation, then this needs championing by more than one person (see Dilemma 10). It needs to be shaped, critiqued, organized, implemented and finished in at least

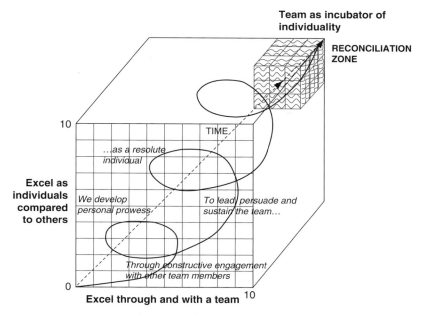

Team as incubator of individuality

RECONCILIATION ZONE

10

TIME

…as a resolute individual

Excel as individuals compared to others

We develop personal prowess

To lead, persuade and sustain the team…

Through constructive engagement with other team members

0

Excel through and with a team 10

DILEMMA 10 Achieving and excelling as individuals vs. achieving and excelling through teams

a prototype form. The urging of a whole team can sometimes accomplish this, the lone inventor rarely can.

One reason why so many innovations are start-ups is that the solo, inventive individual within the corporation is in a very weak position. Corporations are structured around current tasks and around serving current customers. They resist being re-structured for a different purpose. The individual has almost no chance of prevailing unless s/he gets a team to champion the new initiative. This is the rationale behind TIP's strong emphasis on team-working.

Teams are also needed to launch start-ups. It is a rare innovator who is strong in every aspect of launching a new product and the key skills must be assembled. This is why the helix for Dilemma 10 first moves to the right to engage would-be members in a joint, constructive enterprise. A team is small enough to respect the individuality of each member, even to support and develop this. It is capable of building up the

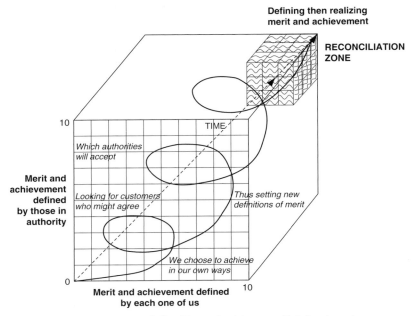

DILEMMA 11 Merit defined by authorities vs. self-defined merit

personal prowess of its most innovative individuals and promoting their ideas. Indeed, individuality, properly understood, grows out of successful social contacts, so that teams can actually incubate the ideas and the individuality of key persons (see the reconciliation zone). It is essential for the innovator to have a team self-organizing around the thrust of his or her venture. Once a team is in place things begin to happen.

The final dilemma in our questionnaire was pursuing the definition of merit. Was this merit as defined by authorities presiding over a meritocracy or merit as defined by the innovative individual? We have argued that unless merit is self-defined it is not truly innovative, self-expressive or self-fulfilling. The schema is set out in the diagram for Dilemma 11.

Here we are fairly confident that self-definition must precede the pursuit of merit and achievement, so the helix first moves to the right and participants are invited to 'state their dream'. Once a purpose has been defined you must win over customers to your idea of merit, then

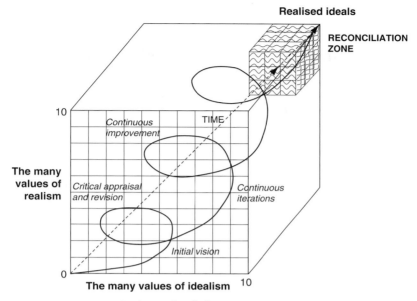

DILEMMA 12 Realizing the ideal

dream further before getting authorities to accept your definition and judge you accordingly. In this reconciliation zone you have both defined and then realized merit and achievement. You have engaged authorities on your own terms.

Thus all eleven questions and dilemmas have harped on the theme of taking an ideal and making this real. We can summarize the impact of this chapter by considering how ideals are realized. It is vital to begin by seeing things not as they are but as they might be, 'to think of things that never were and ask, "Why not?"'

Hence we begin with the initial vision of a changed reality at bottom right (see Dilemma 12). We then critique this re-visioning being as realistic as we can be, and through continuous improvement, grounded in reality testing, we bring an imaginative concept into being as a realized ideal. The wavy pattern in the reconciliation zone is there to remind us that ultimately boundaries collapse. Wave-forms achieve constructive interference and their joint performance peaks. The realized ideal evokes our admiration. This is what life is all about.

8 'It is only the Hawthorne Effect'

People often stumble over the truth, but then they pick themselves up and hurry along as if nothing had happened.

Winston Churchill

There is some danger that people reading this book could make the error to which Churchill refers. Critics of this experiment will say this is 'nothing but the Hawthorne Effect'.[1] There are indeed parallels.

In the famous Hawthorne Experiment[2] in the late 1920s, a group of female factory workers were placed in an experimental setting and there assembled telephone relays. It was a formal experiment in which key changes in their environment, 'independent variables', would supposedly alter the women's output, 'dependent variables'. Changes in illumination, the height of seats and tables, rest periods, food and money were all tried, but the women's productivity steadily increased over time regardless of the variables and remained as high when all the variables were removed. The conclusion was that the women were treated with greater courtesy and consideration than usual, that they had grown to like the researchers, had guessed that these wanted higher productivity and had given it to them.

While Hawthorne has been extremely influential in management studies and is regarded as having (accidentally) shown the way to improved practice, it has fared nothing like as well as a piece of research. Among those concerned with the methodology of experimentation it is thought to be a 'bad experiment'. Its failure as an experiment stems from two sources. The subjects of the experiment came to like the researchers. The academics treated the women as they would colleagues at their university of junior status. However, this was not at all how immigrant working women and factory hands were usually treated in American industry. What the researchers regarded as normal, courteous interaction was not 'normal' at all at Western Electric in those days. Immigrants were pouring into America and could be dismissed at a moment's notice and replaced. Noting that the foreman 'upset' the women, the researchers kept him away.

Because of the affection that broke out accidentally between the researchers and the experimental subjects, the women, knowing that higher productivity was the purpose of the exercise, provided this for the researchers. They might also have wanted to establish that improved working conditions led to improved productivity. This could help their colleagues left behind in the factory.

One might think that such development would be a cause for rejoicing. How nice for entrepreneurs and managers that their employees would reciprocate concern by working more effectively! But purists among researchers regard it as illegitimate for subjects to know the true purpose of what they are doing and doubly illegitimate for subjects to contrive a successful outcome because the experimental conditions are better than what they have known before. There were, in fact, several parallels between the Hawthorne Experiment and the Singapore Experiment. It was our awareness of this that gave our book its sub-title. The fact that the women knew about the purpose of the experiment as did members of our two programmes is one similarity. That both the women and our students wanted the experiment to succeed, and joined together to help it do so, was another similarity.

If we consider the eleven dilemmas and grids on which we measured progress, these also had similarities to Hawthorne. The designed structure of the factory floor was intellectual and cerebral. The engineers had designed it all in advance for workers to operate 'efficiently'. Conditions were lonely and emotionally bleak. The Relay Test Room was emotionally far more satisfying (Dilemma 1). As the independent variables were found to fail repeatedly, the researchers actually enquired of the women why they were working better and the women stated their own beliefs (Dilemma 2). Within the test room a family atmosphere was created, in which there was conviviality with anniversaries celebrated (Dilemma 3). Their activity, defined as an experiment, was tentative and playful with productivity scores given at the end of each day (Dilemma 4). What began as a narrow pursuit of social engineering became transformed into a Human Relations Movement (Dilemma 5).

While the researchers looked only at facts and productivity indices, the women created relationships of greater rapport with everyone concerned (Dilemma 6). The researchers' single-minded pursuit of truth was qualified by the practical accomplishment of the women's higher productivity (Dilemma 7). While the researchers remained doggedly rational and sceptical, it was the combination of new circumstances that wrought the real difference (Dilemma 8). While the researchers worshipped at the altar of science, it was the women who showed that Nature could be altered (Dilemma 9).

The women were taken out of the individualized and alienating structure of the factory, where individual performance is measured against standards, and put into a team whose combined productivity was measured (Dilemma 10). Finally, the researchers who had defined merit for these women gave up this attempt and let them re-define it for themselves (Dilemma 11).

How comes it that an experiment which was credited with creating whole new disciplines, Human Resource Management, Organization Development and Organizational Learning, not to mention HR departments in corporations and the Tavistock Institute for Human Relations, among others, could have had its origins in a 'bad experiment', whose practices have been copied here? What is it about the attitude and rules of mainstream social science which regards this inspiring event with deep suspicion and disapproval? In order to understand this verdict we need to examine five issues.[3]

1. The dilemmas of experimental psychology.
2. Attempts to overcome that dilemma inflict it on experimental subjects.
3. The findings of experimental psychology selectively illuminate the pathologies rather than the virtues of mankind.
4. Is the Prisoners' Dilemma Game an answer to our objection or a part of the problem?
5. We need revised methods to understand innovation.

I. THE DILEMMAS OF EXPERIMENTAL PSYCHOLOGY
The social sciences in their quest for respectability try to ape the natural 'hard' sciences, especially nineteenth-century experimental physics. This deals with dead physical objects which are the effects caused by the Experimenter. S/he represents the 'independent variable' and the objects being studied are the 'dependent variables'. The Experimenter makes unilateral changes in the independent variable and predicts and controls the reactions of the dependent variables in public space, shared with other researchers and replicable by them. The appropriate attitude is one of dispassion and 'objectivity', a word derived from the lifeless objects being observed.

But serious dilemmas arise when you are dealing not with dead objects but live subjects who respond to you. Human conduct is governed by social norms. Were you to be honest with your experimental subjects and say to them, 'I seek to manipulate your behaviour and override your own freedom. I aim to make your conduct entirely predictable and controllable by me', then you would be likely to get a frosty answer, if not outright rebellion. This truth cannot be told.

If experimental subjects do not like the hypothesis being tested, they will contrive to defeat it. For example, the hypothesis that 'Jews cannot tolerate as much pain as Gentiles' is defeated by Jewish subjects tolerating a lot more pain and perhaps by Gentiles deliberately tolerating less. It is a nasty hypothesis and experimental subjects suffer to eliminate it. Similarly if subjects actually like the hypothesis, as they did in the Hawthorne Experiment and in the Singapore Experiment, then they may try to make sure it succeeds. In both cases the experiment is said to be 'distorted' by live subjects guessing what its purpose is and making choices accordingly.

This leaves psychological experimenters with only one option as they see it, which is to deceive experimental subjects as to the purpose of the experiment. This is done routinely, but there are three notorious series of experiments, the Asch-Crutchfield Conformity experiments,[4]

Stanley Milgram's Obedience experiments[5] and Zimbardo's Prison experiment.[6] I shall briefly summarize and review all three.

In conformity experiments the experimenter pretends that he wants the help of subjects in tests of perception. He shows them lines of comparative length and/or circles of comparative volume and invites their verdicts. What in fact is happening is that everyone in the room is conspiring to deliver a contrived consensus save one whose willingness to go along with this lie is being assessed. The real purpose is to see whether that one person, deprived of support by the others in the room, will give an honest judgement or simply conform to avoid being conspicuous or discovering that his/her judgement is faulty. The number of subjects conforming was found to be a majority and the experimenters were duly shocked.

Milgram's Obedience experiments proceeded on similar lines. Subjects volunteered and were then paid to conduct a pseudo-experiment, ostensibly about 'the effect of pain on learning'. The volunteer had to administer pain to another 'volunteer' who in fact was in league with the experimenter. The volunteer deliberately failed the memory tests and was given escalating 'electric shocks' after each mistake which he greeted with feigned cries of pain. This was the regimen to which the volunteer had agreed in advance. After cries and groans from the 'victim', after mention of a weak heart and after failing to respond at all, the volunteer was told 'the experiment must continue' and that failure to answer was equivalent to a mistake. The shocks continued to be administered even after the victim seemed to have lapsed into unconsciousness. Of course, the real purpose of the experiment, which would have been defeated had the subjects known the truth, was to discover how many people would obey orders to torture another human being in the name of science and its authority.

The Zimbardo experiment occurred several years later at UC Berkeley. Students in a class were chosen by lot to play the roles of guards and prisoners in a pretend jail. The 'guards' were told to discipline the 'prisoners' who did not cooperate in their own incarceration. Several quite shocking incidents transpired, so serious that the experiment had to be terminated early lest the university be held liable.

All three experiments prevented experimental subjects from knowing what the experimenter predicted and sought to establish. In the first two cases the trickery was elaborate. In Zimbardo's case he would have got a different result if he had told the students he was hoping to discover how badly one group would behave when they had control over another and the Experimenter had control over them all. Note that the false definition of the experiment accorded with the social norms of the university, while the real purpose did not. You do not manipulate people by lying to them in normal intercourse. In all cases, but especially in the conformity experiments, where it was measured, anxiety rose sharply within subjects when their eyesight or judgement was challenged unanimously. By conforming the subjects lowered their anxiety, but their minds must have been confused. Subjects found themselves agreeing with the contrived consensus that 'Free Speech being a privilege not a right, the authorities may withdraw it'. This was an interesting insight into how easily democracy is subverted.

Anxiety was also reported by Milgram – subjects found themselves in the appalling dilemma of administering electric shocks to 'victims' too agonized to answer. They did not want to continue and begged the psychologist to end it, but he monotonously intoned 'the experiment must continue'. They sweated, lamented and protested, but a majority did as they were told. In the Zimbardo experiment the 'guards' especially were greatly upset by their own conduct once debriefed.

My argument is not that these researchers were somehow villainous persons, quite the contrary in fact. Their sadness at what they discovered seems completely genuine. The pleasure with which they describe the humane and creative personalities of those who refused to continue with the experiment or told the truth is equally persuasive. These 'refuseniks' were the heroes of the hour. All the social scientists wrote strongly worded essays on the evils of conformity, obedience to authority and the unilateral powers of prison guards. Zimbardo gave evidence at the US inquiry into the Abu Ghraib prison scandal in Iraq, citing his own research as foreshadowing this tragedy. His horror at man's inhumanity to man is clearly genuine. Many US psychologists are Jewish and their fear that the Holocaust might be repeated is understandable.

2. ATTEMPTS TO OVERCOME THAT DILEMMA INFLICT IT ON EXPERIMENTAL SUBJECTS

The Experimenter's own dilemma is that his subjects are alive, conscious, intelligent and purposive, unlike physical objects, and he needs to defeat these qualities in them. He deems himself the 'independent variable', but so do they! Social norms among consenting adults assume that both parties exercise volition. The Experimenter needs to take this volition away, without warning his subjects that this is being done, or they might revolt! This is why deceit is chosen. It is the only way out of the dilemma. If they knew, they might comply with a negative hypothesis or defy it. The unexamined assumption is that you are more 'scientific' if your subjects do not know what you are doing. You do not *want* to lie to them necessarily and you do not enjoy it, but you more nearly approximate physics if you reduce them to 'naïve' pieces of clay that are 'caused to behave' in a certain way by your unilateral manipulations of the key variables.

Dilemma produces anxiety as we have seen. The Experimenter reduces anxiety by taking the hard sciences as a model, but then dumps the anxiety which s/he has avoided upon the heads of experimental subjects. They must face the prospect that their eyes deceive them and/or that their civic education was mistaken. When told by the university to 'help social science' they find themselves torturing people, or so they believe. When playing at being guards they plot to subjugate and humiliate prisoners and disgust themselves in the process.

Note the conjunction of several variables that characterize totalitarian systems. There is the Great Lie as expounded by Joseph Goebbels, but artfully disguised as consensus. There is cruelty sanctioned by a higher ideal, that of learning. There is a Führer-principle called the Independent Variable, which forbids genuine consensus lest subjects get their hands on the steering wheel, and there is gross inequality between the parties, so that subjects are trapped in dilemmas occasioning severe anxiety. Have we not encountered this before in various dictatorial regimes?

What one looks for in vain in the writings of these well-meaning psychologists is the admission that the experimental conditions themselves contributed to the shocking outcomes. They do not seem to understand that they created the conditions under which these pathological behaviours occurred. They may have been honestly determined to be as 'scientific' as possible but they largely failed to see what this entailed and how they induced their subjects to behave like this. There is, of course, a serious fallacy at the base of experimental psychology. Experimenters want to avoid eliciting the behaviour they are searching for and they want to avoid defiance of such elicitation. This is why they lie. But if they fondly imagine that they have avoided a self-fulfilling prophecy they are totally mistaken. Subjects made acutely anxious and trapped between their own agendas and the hidden agendas of the Experimenter will do terrible things to reduce inner pain. Punishing or otherwise controlling another person is a pain-reducing stratagem by the aggressor.

The whole notion that keeping subjects 'naïve' while you plot is going to stop your hypothesis fulfilling itself is absurd. Human subjects will react whatever you do and typically they will react in kind. You cannot turn them into passive objects however hard you try. If you approach them with dispassion and a clipboard they will reciprocate your conduct. A smile will elicit a smile. If you lie to them, they will become confused and anxious and your lie will come full circle back to you, in the form of outrageous conduct. You will discover your own inhumanity in them, without grasping that it was you who put it there. We desperately need experiments in truth-telling and attempts to develop people.

Experimenters write articles in which they admire those who resisted them, who told the truth in the conformity experiment, who threw the money back into the faces of Milgram's researchers and even insisted on freeing the victims from their restraints. They call such persons 'Independents'. They were, as we might expect, more creative, more compassionate, more socially confident, more egalitarian and more liberal, as revealed by personality tests. But the researchers did not pause to ask themselves, 'What is it about my experiment that makes outstanding personalities want to wreck it?' If the only way you can discover human virtue is through those who threaten to wreck your laboratory, what does that tell you about the methods you are using? Was their anger perhaps justified? Had they found the experimenters out?

3. THE FINDINGS OF EXPERIMENTAL PSYCHOLOGY SELECTIVELY ILLUMINATE THE PATHOLOGIES RATHER THAN THE VIRTUES OF MANKIND

Unfortunately personality-testing is regarded by strict experimentalists as irredeemably 'soft', while the findings on torturers are commendably 'hard'. While we have 'scientific' experiments on conformity, obedience, compliant cruelty and the exercise of unilateral power over powerless persons, we have virtually no experiments on compassion, understanding, playfulness, humour, innovation and creativity. It is surely obvious why. These simply do not manifest themselves in the presence of attempts to manipulate and deceive. They are the products of passion, not dispassion, caring not cruelty, of being the origin of ideas, not the passive result of others' machinations.

But the harm done by the selective unveiling of misconduct, while claiming that this is 'human nature', not the result of 'scientific' tinkering, is only part of it. We need to ask what is *not* discovered by such experiments. You do not and cannot discover what happens when subjects are told the truth, when they grow attached to one another, when they are exposed to a highly stimulating ecosystem, when they are invited to become independent variables themselves, when the search for discovery is a joint enterprise shared with researchers and the excitement of the hunt infects everyone.

It has always been easier to count fragments than whole patterns of culture. 'Scientific' methodology reduces phenomena to pieces so that it can enumerate these easily. Alas, no one is able to put Humpty-Dumpty together again and we have a psychology of smashed debris beyond the capacities of men, much less horses, to re-assemble. We speak of data (things given) but these are really *capta*, things seized and held. No wonder the human image arising from these captured parts resembles Dr Frankenstein's Monster.

4. IS THE PRISONERS' DILEMMA GAME AN ANSWER TO OUR OBJECTION OR A PART OF THE PROBLEM?

We have not yet mentioned experimental psychology's 'answer' to the objections made so far, the Prisoners' Dilemma Game.[7] This game has won favour because two experimental subjects compete with each other in a 'game'. They consent to do this and they are not lied to and they interact with each other as equals rather than being directly manipulated by the Experimenter. Literally tens of thousands of articles have been published on this experiment over half a century.

The context is as follows. Two prisoners have been apprehended and are suspects for the commission of a crime. They are confronted by the Attorney General of their state and questioned separately. They each have a 'choice'. Whoever betrays the other prisoner first will get off free, while the other prisoner will be severely punished. If both refuse to talk they will get a reduced sentence, because the more serious charge remains unproven. In short there are three pay-offs:

(a) Betray your fellow prisoner when he is sticking by you.
(b) Refuse to betray and trust that your fellow prisoner does likewise.
(c) Refuse to betray and be betrayed by him.

By far the 'best' outcome is (a). A compromise of sorts is (b), and the worst possible outcome is (c).

We have used the concept of dilemma throughout this book. But *our* dilemmas are potentially reconcilable and the reconciliations create wealth. In the Prisoners' Dilemma Game, the dilemma is carefully constructed so as to be irreconcilable. Win, lose or compromise are the only choices and the subjects cannot escape from the 'game' they are playing any more than they can get through the bars of their cells. Keep faith with your fellow prisoner and you could go to jail for years because he betrayed you. We might ask, what prevents the dilemma from being reconciled like others in this book? The answer is the unequal power of the Attorney General and the prisoners he holds captive. The system of betray, be betrayed or compromise has been deliberately used to break them down, confuse them and to extort confessions. The experimental subjects are prisoners in every sense of the word, for whom the highest pay-off is unilateral betrayal of someone who trusts you. What prevents the dilemma from being reconciled is its imposition of superior force by the State's Attorney. We are back to the climax of *1984* where the two lovers Winston and Julia are imprisoned and he pleads, 'Do it to Julia! Not me!' She pleads, 'Don't do it to me, do it to somebody else, do it to [Winston].' They later reflect, 'Under the spreading chestnut tree I sold you and you sold me'.[8]

One is tempted to say that it takes an experimental psychologist to think up such clever forms of oppression, in which prisoners essentially inform upon and punish each other and those who preside over it all keep their hands clean. Presumably psychologists are helping us deal with the world as we find it, but for how many of us is the world a prison cell from which we can escape only by betraying fellow captives? There are indeed visions of capitalism which state that you must exploit or be exploited. This appears to be such a situation. If economics is the Dismal Science, what is *this*?

5. WE NEED REVISED METHODS TO UNDERSTAND INNOVATION

The methods used in this book were admittedly unorthodox, but we trapped, imprisoned and coerced no one. The subjects knew what we wanted to discover because we had told them many times. They could have lied to us, offering us false comfort, but we seriously doubt that they did so because the dangers of false comfort had been impressed upon them many times. The market 'out there' would punish us far more severely than they could. False comfort is the enemy of innovation. They had to be tough with each other and surely with us too? The idea that respondents would not tell us the truth as they saw it, after our telling them that timely criticism drives improvement, strikes us as most improbable.

The whole programme was far too important for them, for NTU, for Singapore and for China for them to lie about it. The consequences of any flaws would be visited on future classes. As pointed out at the beginning of Chapter 5 our respondents had been out in the unforgiving world of innovation for at least some months and up to five years before receiving our questionnaire. Had we neglected to warn them of something that had later ruined them, they would surely have told us this unequivocally! Given the high failure rates for most start-ups, their temptation to blame us when things went wrong was surely strong. So, far from our respondents being too positive, we risked a backlash from those disappointed by failure. If they were not steeled to truth they were wasting their time and ours by responding at all.

In any case our results were far from perfect and show room for substantial improvement on our part. Just under half the respondents from Singapore and from the PRC reached the reconciliation zone, the wavy square in our grids. This means that 50 to 60 per cent did not. We have much more to do. Our failings were brought home to us. Clearly more than half our respondents did not report to us what we wanted to hear and what they knew we wanted.

If you cannot trust respondents to give you honest answers, however disappointing these are, then subjects like innovation, creativity, entrepreneurship and psycho-social development must remain for ever beyond the reach of social science. Virtue consists of integral patterns, while lying, coercing, imprisoning and preventing dilemmas being reconciled consigns virtuous conduct to outraged protestors. Perhaps this is one reason why social science students were foremost among the rebels of the late sixties and early seventies.

9 The programme that cannot stand still

If you are teaching innovation and entrepreneurship then you can never be satisfied with the existing courses and programmes. This is so because you need to model what you are teaching, take similar risks and explore similar kinds of new territory. You cannot expect students to experiment if you are not experimenting too. It is essential that new efforts be mounted on the top of earlier efforts like a fresh performance on a stage, so that each successive accomplishment transcends the previous one and teaches you something you did not know before. If students have their hearts in their mouths then teachers should be modelling the same kind of risk-taking. Let us recall that the TIP course was in part the students' shared project, something they must help to make into a success. If the course is not genuinely experimental, why should the students get excited?

A major new theme in the course is the introduction of digital media, which in turn has a number of ramifications. I shall discuss these in turn.

(a) Film as an ongoing narrative drama
(b) The digital case clearing house
(c) Digital and other prototypes
(d) The City of Digital Dreams
(e) Whole system change and alternative futures
(f) Beyond the zero-sum game

The remarkable development over the last decade of digital media technology is the background of all six of these issues. Just as the personal computer put at the individual's fingertips the power formerly wielded by large corporations only a few years earlier, so now are Hollywood's resources, formerly unavailable, coming to many homes and offices in the land, although the skills to exploit these must still be learned. NTC has included as its Deputy Director Ray Abelin, an ex-Hollywood director, who has set out to see what digital media might do to expand entrepreneurship and innovation.

(A) FILM AS AN ONGOING NARRATIVE DRAMA

We saw in our discussion of the Hawthorne Experiment in Chapter 8 that one reason why the young women worked better and better was that they found themselves within a narrative with interested spectators all around them. As their productivity climbed so did the rapt attention of their audience and the number of distinguished visitors peering into the room. This must have convinced the women of an important truth that what they were engaged upon could have momentous consequences. A long story had begun to unwind.

Anyone who is genuinely innovative in any field is on the leading edge of knowledge and is entitled to feel a sense of drama and excitement. This would actually be rather more authentic than the excitement generated by all but the best films. This is because excitement-for-entertainment is typically contrived, while excitement over something genuinely new (which could include films) is part of the innovative process. It follows that to make dramatic films of such exploits conveys to an audience what it actually feels like to be on the cutting edge of change, to make a real difference and to find meaning in what had hitherto been a humdrum life. A digital record of your own trials, tribulations and triumphs is a way of telling other potential innovators what it is like. Narrative film shares with exploration and discovery an eventful story line, a series of crises and frustrations, leading on occasion to a vindication of the courage and effort involved.

To this end Ray Abelin has shot a film of the students' 'learning journey' including the Outward Bound bonding exercise and travels to Seattle, Washington, the Bay Area, Stanford University, etc. The film has an obvious use in recruiting the next intake but far more important in our estimation is the general feeling of being 'on stage' and helping to make history. A learning journey is something from which you return changed. To record it on film is to highlight its importance and make it memorable.

Directing a film is an interesting metaphor for an innovative kind of organization. The really successful director cannot tell people exactly what to do. The set is full of professional actors and technical specialists. Vivien Leigh, being an attractive woman, probably knows better than her director how Scarlett O'Hara would behave if she wanted something from a man. Actors and actresses need to interpret their roles and be free to improvise and experiment. What the best directors do is keep telling the story, since scenes are not shot in sequence, so constant reminders of what is happening now and why are necessary to get people in the mood. In a very real sense the director is responsible for the culture of the set and the ongoing sense of drama in which everyone must play their part. Get this culture of innovation right and the team self-organizes around the narrative theme.

The *Learning Journey* film is professionally modest, good enough for the classroom and to show friends where you have been, but not of broadcast quality. But Ray Abelin, with this author as the narrator, has recently shot a $2 million documentary film using the latest Sony high-definition camera and entitled *Innovation and the Fate of Nations*, which traces the history of ideas from Cambridge University to Massachusetts in the wake of John Harvard, one of the 'Cambridge Men' who brought higher learning to New England. Later in the twentieth century it traces Lee Kuan Yew from the law faculty at Cambridge University to the creation of the Singaporean constitution and his leadership of that country. The role of this and future films is to create a narrative context into which the TIP programmes fit. Why must nations innovate or decline? What is at stake in programmes like this? How do West and East differ in their approach to innovation? What is the role of science and ideas in the development of national cultures? Were programmes like this to work, what would the implications be?

The film starts with the dawn of innovation. Pharaohs and Chinese Emperors, who deemed themselves god-like, were attempting to deny their own mortality. They had themselves buried among deathless arte-facts of great beauty, playthings for an afterlife. The film tracks two revolutions, the radical scepticism of Sir Isaac Newton with its dismissal of what could not be directly experienced by the senses, along with the clean sweep of ornate religion demanded by the Puritans, who sought for truth in written texts not graven images and who justified themselves through works. It is vital that students see themselves as the inheritors of these struggles.

The film also illustrates the East Asian strategies of 'catch-up capitalism'. One such strategy consists of first sub-contracting the work of a Western multinational and then gradually hollowing this corporation out by doing more and more. For example, Flextronics in Singapore began by making circuit boards for companies like Hewlett Packard. This contributed to HP's profits and improved their assets-to-profit ratio. Then Flextronics asked to make the motherboards, a somewhat more complex task. Again, profits improved. Why should HP bother with supply-chain management and logistics? Flextronics could do that too. Finally they got to make the intelligence within the printers and computers themselves. This is how East Asian cultures compete 'cooperatively', climbing the steps of the knowledge ladder one by one as they learn, while making sure their customer profits. There is only one flaw. The host corpo-ration is having its core competence eaten away even as its financials look better. Is profitability a Moloch to which survival skills are being sacrificed?

Films like this attempt to place innovation on the world stage, impressing audiences with the urgency of the quest. If Newton could see further than others as he did because he 'stood on the shoulders of giants', then so can we. It is not just the heritage of Chinese immigrant entrepreneurs that programme participants have to thank, important although this is, but knowledge and information spanning the globe and how this was wrought originally.

(B) THE DIGITAL CASE CLEARING HOUSE

One of the most fundamental pillars of business scholarship and legal studies is the case method of learning. This stands as a testament to the uniqueness of every new achievement in the creation of wealth, a reminder that no two cases are quite the same and that we can be ambushed by ingenuity at any moment. It reminds us to generalize cautiously and watch for the unprecedented. It is also a useful exercise in humility. Innovation is less a product of business schools themselves than the product of practitioners out there in the business environment practising arts of innovation.

The Harvard Case Clearing House can typically provide a case description within months of any new development. It is the major process by which educators keep up with events and it is part of the Anglo-American common law tradition, that each case is a precedent and judgments are made on the basis of similarities and principles. The higher the level of innovation the more important become the case studies because few generalizations hold. But are written cases studied in the evenings and discussed the next day in classrooms enough? To read about a case is not to live it, but to escape the pressures of real events. It is too abstract, too cerebral, too much at arm's length. Cases of attempted innovation are by their nature dramatic, even melodramatic. The entrepreneur stakes his/her home, reputation, friends, relatives, career, judgement and future on an outcome more often negative than positive. Among the victims could be the education of children and the savings of parents.

This is heady stuff. It tears at the emotions and brings delight or disappointment. It deserves to be taught via a medium that pulls you into the drama and immerses you in the thick of events. Filmed narratives are very effective at doing this. Something must be done to prepare technopreneurs for the pain and the tension inherent in their pursuits. Can they think quickly when aroused? You can stop the film with every new crisis and ask 'what now?'

Simulations are very important in this regard. Many entrepreneurs encounter serial failures and this process is agonizing, causing many to give up. But the more simulations of pain you can show on screen, the more common causes of failure you can depict, the quicker the innovators learn without suffering personally. These are a couple of dozen errors that the would-be entrepreneurs won't be making because they have been dramatically forewarned. This was the whole point of classic drama in ancient Greece. You face the great crises of the human condition in your imagination rather than in reality. When the audience swept up in a shared catharsis weep for Medea's murdered children, they vow not to let quarrels with their partners spiral out of control. Suffer in your imagination and you may stop yourself suffering in reality. It is said that we learn most from negative feedback, from events that surprise and confound us. Such incidents can haunt us for years. But it is better to experience negative feedback on stage and in simulation than have a shock that wipes you out commercially and assures you have no allies left. If we are not to make the same mistake twice, let the first time we make it be simulated on-screen.

The making of a film that culminates with the Singapore Experiment's place in the larger scheme of things is, of course, yet another entrepreneurial venture, a 'case' in and of itself, occurring in the midst of the programme where everyone can see. Whether this film is effective, how it can be marketed and how much money it might make are all subjects to be discussed by the ongoing class members. A film may be the most entrepreneurial venture of all, spelling boom or bust, triumph or tribulation, all within a very short time. So much is at stake that the principals live off their nerves. Rather in the manner of *The Treasure of the Sierra Madre*, success can lead to a spell of 'gold fever' that destroys the adventurers themselves. It would be hard to think of an object lesson in innovation better than making a film in the midst of those learning to envision possibilities. They can witness at first hand the ratcheting up of hope, shadowed by suspicion and despair.

Quite apart from filmed cases for instructional purposes, there is an argument for entrepreneurial dramas as a form of entertainment. A culture gets the heroes it deserves and wants. Where filmed cases of entrepreneurial drama are widely enjoyed those hopeful of succeeding in a way their culture celebrates will come forward. We need role models of technopreneurs-in-action. We need exponents of the values which their culture most admires and portraying these is a powerful stimulus to activity.

Negotiations are currently taking place between NTC and Harvard Business School Publishing on the filming of recent cases of innovation which have dramatic potential. These could also be used for distance learning. Filmed interviews with outstanding academics in this field, Professors Clayton Christiansen, Howard Stevenson (President of HBS Publishing) and Theresa Amabile, with Lord Eatwell, Master of Queens' College, with Hermann Hauser, inventor of the ink-jet printer, and with Gordon Edge, inventor of the hydrogen fuel cell battery, have been recorded, and it is hoped that a shared archive can be created of fresh perspectives on the innovative process.

(C) DIGITAL AND OTHER PROTOTYPES

Many innovative products benefit greatly from prototypes, images of the product which those developing it have in mind.[1] When being briefed by customers the latter may know little of what they really want until the prototype is shown to them. Something to look at jointly and to be modified as required, until agreement is reached, can be invaluable. Funding a venture depends critically on the enthusiasm which is likely to be engendered by the product. While a business plan may be essential this has limited use in rendering a product attractive to all concerned or conveying its appeal to consumers. Rather like a written case, the business plan may be too prosaic to appeal.

Plans are afoot at NTC to have the Engineering School supply soft plastics that can be readily shaped into the forms of envisaged products and later harden to retain their shape. A prototyping lab is being readied where computer simulations and CAD can be run so as to test ideas-in-the-making. These are able to winkle out a product's elementary errors or features displeasing to stakeholders.

But by the far greatest possibilities lie with digital prototypes. Here vivid moving images of the product, viewed from every side and every angle, can be prepared and projected onto a screen. An almost exact replica of the vision in the minds of the innovators can be conveyed to those whose support is needed. The image will usually cost a mere fraction of the finished product and could in many cases be computer-generated, with corrections also generated by the computer. Agreement is reached at far lower cost by successive approximations.

Yet this is only the beginning. The product may have to be repaired, maintained and serviced and how to do this can be demonstrated. The product may alter the patterns of customer and consumer behaviour and the advantages of doing this can be depicted. The product may be modular, capable of fitting into a larger system, and this too needs to be illustrated. It may leave users better off and make possible new activities. Digital media can show many of these ramifications. Of course in such cases the digital image is not a product in its own right, like a film would be, but rather a stepping-stone to a greatly improved product system. No wonder that the government of Singapore has created Fusionopolis, a cluster of down-town businesses specializing in digital media of many kinds.[2] Clusters bring together people of similar persuasions who often meet in coffee shops and pavement restaurants to generate the Silicon Valley phenomenon of 'coffee bar creativity', wherein two or more persons working on the same kind of problem discover common ground. Clusters are not simply convenient through the proximity of similar pursuits – they make serendipitous connections more likely to occur. Digital prototypes have the potential to be catalysts within such clusters, showcasing the variety of ideas.

(D) THE CITY OF DIGITAL DREAMS

One of the long-cherished ideals of capitalism is that of a 'market-place for ideas', where the best of ideas compete with each other for our delectation. In this way human ingenuity will get its due reward. Unfortunately it rarely works out that way. Some of the best ideas may fail for lack of adequate resources and some of the most abundant resources may fail for lack of good ideas. Ideas spread by word of mouth are easily stolen and the real genius too often loses out. You can of course patent your ideas but this is a laborious process. Ninety per cent of patents fail to make money and their purpose is often defensive, to stop others engaging in this line of research. Japan currently files the most patents of any country but is not generally considered the most innovative nation.

But by using digital media a market-place for ideas, capable of dramatic enactment, could become a reality. We could create Museums of the Future, wherein the shape of things to come could be displayed and a royalty extracted from anyone who had seen it and then provided the resources to test-market it. In addition to written descriptions of the product, typical of a patent application, easily accessible moving pictures would show the product in action. Singapore with its Fusionopolis might be a suitable site for the City of Digital Dreams.

Yet as Tan Teng-Kee points out the idea is not merely to showcase what Singapore has created, but to open up a market-place to the whole world and have them display their ideas in a global clearing house situated in Singapore, a place where venture capitalists and innovative persons could gather and meet amidst a galaxy of moving images. Historically Singapore became one of the world's first free-trade areas and an open market. Thanks to Sir Stamford Raffles it became very much more than a strategic port city on the route from India to China. Goods were off-loaded and sold to traders, merchants and consumers from the whole of Asia. A market-place for imagined future products is a real possibility.

(E) WHOLE SYSTEM CHANGE AND ALTERNATIVE FUTURES

We may need to alter our focus from being product- or thing-based to being system-based. More and more 'products' are on closer examination elements in a larger system. Even automobiles are connected via global positioning to satellites orbiting earth. It is becoming difficult to tell where a system ends. Our current view of innovation often resembles a collision derby. A new product races onto the circuit and succeeds in demolishing vehicles already there. Destructive or disruptive innovation is a popular term.[3] One has to ask whether this is the best way to introduce changes. We are moving from an environment where product vies with product to one where system vies with system and we need to make broad choices as to which system we prefer. In the depiction of whole systems and how they might be expected to work if designed and installed, digital imagery is essential. We are talking of alternative futures.

Take the hydrogen car, which may yet reduce our dangerous addiction to oil. If we regard it as another product it has little chance of competing. Where would it be fuelled? How would it be maintained, repaired and serviced? Would drivers have to be re-educated? If, when garaged, it can be attached to the domestic utility system and supplement this, which is possible, what savings would this engender? Obviously such a vehicle would require whole system change and what we would be buying is not one car but an alternative future for energy and transport systems. We already have a tentative example of this in the eco-city adjoining Shanghai. Our present system of push and shove between products is not environmentally friendly. The Los Angeles Light Railway was closed down because the automobile and tyre lobbies pushed for this, but they did no favours to Los Angeles which is now among the most gridlocked and polluted cities in America. A future that included an optimal mix of public and private transport would have been much better.

We need digital images of different futures together with estimated paybacks, with coherent scenarios of what such a world would look like. We must see these in order to be able to choose wisely. We must be prepared to change multiple variables at the same time to see how these might configure. For example, what might an oil-free environment do for respiratory diseases among older people, for the incidence of childhood asthma, for an increase in tourism, for the longer life of buildings and masonry, for willingness to play outdoors? The calculations are many. But the choice is between whole scenarios and coherent systems which would have to be simulated and digitally enhanced in order for us to understand them. Digital media are not just booming industries in their own right but empower the process of innovation itself.

(F) BEYOND THE ZERO-SUM GAME

According to the fascinating book *NonZero* by Robert Wright,[4] human moral awareness depends crucially on getting beyond the zero-sum game. This is a game of endemic scarcity in which people either win or lose because they are competing for scarce resources. Football, baseball and nearly all spectator sports are zero-sum and the excitement lies in the difference between success and failure. Computer games are a vast digital industry but almost without exception these are zero-sum and very frequently violent, as when you are invited to mow down *untermenschen* by driving a simulated car. Vast sums are expended in teaching our children to fight for scarce resources and liquidate imaginary foes.

But why could there not be a 'synergy game' in which the players exchanged mutual exploitation for constructive engagement? Why cannot we simulate a world where abundance is deliberately constructed by players, that in later pages we describe as an Infinite Game? Lego and the old British game Mechano were infinite games for creative children. Surely this can be done digitally and its entertainment value may be the highest of all. To create is potentially the greatest fulfilment of all.

What we simulate and play we may eventually do. It was William James who said that mankind has yet to discover 'the moral equivalent of war', something with the heady idealisms of war but minus its appalling destruction, waste and misery. To innovate takes courage, dedication, persistence, resilience, imagination, egalitarianism and empathy. Above all it is constructive not destructive. All games are a form of practising. Change your game, change yourself and change the world.

SUMMARY

Digital media give us new opportunities to tell powerful stories. If we tell stories of innovation we can succeed in mobilizing thousands of would-be innovators. We can create a new cultural methodology. A good start would be to create films of our more dramatic business cases and distribute these worldwide. There is genuine drama in all authentic efforts to innovate. Let us imagine the present high failure rate so as not to repeat this. Most new products go through a prototype stage. Digital prototypes can put products through their paces and portray ideas at their most attractive. We could even create a City of Digital Dreams where people gathered to be inspired. The larger and more comprehensive the product system, the more essential it is to have a medium that generates whole new futures, invitations to whole system change. We need to get beyond zero-sum games with their dismal scarcities and rejoice in our capacity to be constructive and originate wealth. This capacity can be taught to us via digital games, simulations of a better future.

10 Innovation and the future of the university

At Harvard University a new campus is being built where a suburb of Boston, Allston, once stood. It stands next to the Harvard Business School on the Boston side of the Charles River. The plans for the campus, which will be as large as the whole of Caltech, have much to teach us about innovation and the future of the university. Assuming that these plans are fulfilled an extraordinarily bold vision of the university at the leading edge of an innovative economy will emerge. The Allston Campus will be inter-disciplinary and project-based. It will consist of cross-disciplinary alliances by two or more Harvard graduate schools who seek to make a novel synthesis between their fields of study. For example, research on the human genome will join forces with the School of Medicine to revolutionize medical diagnosis and treatment. Electronics is likely to join forces with mechanical engineering. Nano-technology will explore possibilities with chemistry and the life sciences. Up to this time seventy proposals for joint working have been received, but they have yet to be judged and the buildings housing them have still to be constructed.

There will be two graduate schools also present on this site, the School of Education and the School of Public Health, both inter-disciplinary by definition, and of course the Harvard Business School is close by. All three have the opportunity to learn from, to coordinate and to utilize what is being developed around them. If we regard Harvard's Allston Campus as the potential shape of the future, which many other universities will come to imitate, then what does this signify? Are these plans consistent with the research findings in Chapters 5 and 6? I shall address these topics under the following headings:

(a) An innovative university requires major institutional changes through the creation of inter-disciplinary, problem-centred projects.

(b) Despite popular misconceptions you cannot 'buy' innovative achievements on the open market, not even by ever larger payments.

(c) The incubator of innovation is the often powerless, cash-strapped primary group of cross-disciplinary experts.

(d) Schools of business may not be the institutions best suited for promoting innovation.

(e) Innovators are the last minority to be fully emancipated.

(A) AN INNOVATIVE UNIVERSITY REQUIRES MAJOR INSTITUTIONAL CHANGES THROUGH THE CREATION OF INTER-DISCIPLINARY, PROBLEM-CENTRED PROJECTS

It is no exaggeration to say that most modern universities are structured in a way that actively prevents many innovative breakthroughs or useful contributions to the problems of society. The political power in contemporary universities typically resides in the deans of various graduate schools. Each graduate school is a fiefdom, a functional 'silo', specializing in particular (sometimes narrow) disciplines, each intent on increasing its own size and influence relative to other schools. Of course, new discoveries often are made within disciplinary boundaries, especially within the hard sciences like physics, chemistry and biology, but this is probably a small fraction of the answers that lie hidden in between the disciplines,[1] areas undiscovered because people who are qualified in more than one discipline are very rare.

We can grasp this more easily if we look at any complex social problem and ask what it would take to solve it. How, for example, might we combat the scourge of drug addiction? We would need chemistry to find us possible substitutes, doctors of medicine to treat addiction and withdrawal, anthropologists to advise on what is clearly a sub-culture and life-style problem, psychologists to advise on the syndrome of chronic dependence, sociologists to throw light upon the *anomie* of users, economists to trace the lavish profits of drug lords, criminologists to throw light on organized crime syndicates, lawyers and government experts to decide whether new legislation would help, political scientists and international relations experts to trace the supply of drugs to failed states like Colombia and Afghanistan, plant scientists to advise on crop eradication and historians to point out the dismal record of failure thus far. Without most of these contributions the solution to the drug problem would have no chance at all. It is common knowledge that 'drug busts' by police only succeed in raising the price of drugs, which assures their fresh supply. What is required is simultaneous inputs from various disciplines into various places in that system.

Yet the likelihood of graduate schools lending their expertise to such composite efforts is very small indeed, given the present institutional structure. Graduate schools like to 'own' the problems they work on. Their rewards go to those who advance the discipline, not to those with minority inputs into world problems. Those who stray to the borders of their discipline are typically punished. Those who cross those borders can expect to fare worse. Being fascinated by innovation, this author has worked for most of his life with inter-disciplinary programmes at universities, which originated in Harvard, Stanford, UC Berkeley, and NTU.[2] The Singapore Experiment itself is the product of an inter-disciplinary centre.

Observing the fate of such programmes has been a saddening but increasingly familiar experience. A sponsor offers money. The university accepts it. Two or more disciplines collaborate in one centre. The centre is evaluated by the schools that originally staffed the operation. It is found to be 'good' but 'not good enough', having been 'contaminated' by the other disciplines. The graduate schools ask for the balance of the funds to revert to them or for the centre to be absorbed into either of the schools. The temporary bridge between the schools collapses. The author has now witnessed this four times. And, of course, it essentially kills any hope of inter-disciplinary dialogue or solutions to the world's problems, or even the capacity of students to grasp wider meanings.

It was George Homans, the Harvard sociologist, who lamented, 'The social sciences became bureaucratised before they ever became useful.' Their usefulness depends on their not imposing a division of labour on social patterns, but this is precisely what bureaucratizing does. The last time the author visited the American Psychological Association it had sixty-seven divisions! There are probably many more today.

Those who operate between disciplines are 'interesting' for many schools but essential to none. When judged by any one school only what has been done for that discipline will count and the rest will be discounted. Those between disciplines are treated as part-timers. At best what they have achieved is 'applied science' lacking the purity of disciplined work. These same problems are present in the Singapore Experiment described in these pages, and its achievements may yet be destroyed. It is currently under the strongest pressure to be taken back into NTU's Business School for which Tan Teng-Kee once worked. When he first launched the programme he received so little help that he spun off the Centre. But now that the programme is gathering plaudits the Business School wants it back! Technopreneurship is a branch of business, it is said. I shall discuss the merits of this claim later in this chapter.

Given the usual fate of inter-disciplinary programmes, Harvard's decision to house them and nurture them in a separate campus given over to fused disciplines is potentially a stroke of genius, likely to change the university for ever. At long last a university has responded to the many crises facing us. Similar initiatives are occurring at Arizona State University under the activist presidency of Michael M. Crow.

(B) DESPITE POPULAR MISCONCEPTIONS YOU CANNOT 'BUY' INNOVATIVE ACHIEVEMENTS ON THE OPEN MARKET, NOT EVEN BY EVER LARGER PAYMENTS

To grasp what Harvard is doing with its new campus we need to challenge a popular misconception that almost anything, including innovative achievements, can be purchased on the open market. According to this view everything has its price and by the simple expedient of paying more you can obtain it. America certainly leads the world in lavish, multi-million-dollar salaries for its top executives and should, by rights, have a near monopoly of the world's most talented persons. In this case logic requires that it is pulling ever further ahead of competing economies, but is this happening? The uncomfortable truth is that economies paying only a fraction of America's salaries are rapidly catching up.

The idea that you can 'buy' innovative achievement runs into a number of snags. When is the multi-million-dollar CEO going to find the time to actually spend his salary, and if he tried to do so would this not slow him down? Surely the more increments of money you receive the less each increment is worth, a concept known as 'marginal utility'? Do we really need more dependents of rich men buying 500 pairs of shoes? Might not the same money paid to employees motivate such persons more? What kind of culture distributes money to where it is least needed and least effective?

But the fallacy goes much deeper than this. As early as 1958 David McClelland reported in *The Achieving Society* that high achievers achieve for achievement's sake, not for money.[3] When he paid for tasks to be done it was those least interested in achievement who improved their performance; high achievers were unaffected by the offer. People achieve because they welcome a challenge to their own powers and want to discover what they can accomplish. The CEO who sells the HQ building, leases it back and adds millions to the balance sheet in the year of his retirement, is clearly one of those low achievers interested largely in money for himself while creating no genuine wealth at all.

High achievers are interested in money according to McClelland but only as it symbolizes what they feel they have achieved, *after* they have achieved it and presumably as a means to achieve still more. What drives high achievers is 'achievement fantasy', visions of their anticipated success among grateful onlookers, the kind of ideals that drove participants in our experiment. Even where top CEOs 'achieve' after a fashion by maintaining a giant corporation on an even keel, they very rarely innovate. The abundant evidence shows that genuine innovation comes from small and medium-sized companies, many of these in the vicinity of universities like Harvard, MIT, Stanford, Cambridge and the University of Texas at Austin. These often tiny companies can afford to pay their founding staff very little, if anything. They live off achievement fantasy and promised shares in anticipated successes. If such persons intended to maximize profits, they must be among the stupidest operators in the whole world. Most such projects fail.

We have only to look at turnover in the Fortune Five Hundred and other indices to note that many big companies are heading south, like Ford and General Motors, while companies unheard of ten years ago are replacing them. The life-span of most corporations is less than the human life-span. They have great difficulty changing as the world changes. They are often doomed Titans. Research by Clayton Christiansen at Harvard[4] has shown that of 129 computer companies built around disc-drives, 109 went bankrupt because they failed to adapt to the ever shrinking size of those disc-drives. In this refusal, they were joined by their customers! A corporation of any great size, despite its wealth and ability to 'buy' talent, is too often fatally inflexible. As innovation speeds up more giants will topple and fall.

It has nothing to do with not wanting to be innovative. Large corporations speak endlessly about being 'entrepreneurial'. They have also enjoyed considerable success in finding and hiring talented persons, but that is where the problem starts. William Shockley developed the transistor at Bell Labs but had to set up his own company to exploit this opportunity. In turn eight employees had to leave Shockley Semiconductor in order to start the Fairchild Corporation. Yet still the lesson was not learned. Fairchild begat 'the Fair Children', including Intel together with several companies whose innovations failed to get a hearing within Fairchild. Eugene Kleiner had to leave Intel in order to found Kleiner Perkins and so on.[5] Xerox PARC also collected geniuses, Steve Jobs amongst them, but they too had to go their own way in order to innovate effectively. These innovators almost certainly had to accept lower salaries as the price of starting again.

By now it has dawned on big corporations that they accidentally discourage innovation. Lego, the Danish toy company, makes it a rule to start new toy ventures at a distance from HQ to reduce interference.[6] Royal Dutch Shell had to end its 'non-traditional business' ventures. When senior executives kept a 'fatherly eye' on these ventures they also charged their time to them. They sank beneath the sheer weight of such concern. Richard Branson's Virgin company has a general rule that no business should grow much above a hundred persons. A unit this size can remain agile. Units whose success makes them larger are cut in half to compete against one another. Innovation requires a small unit with face-to-face relationships on a first-name basis, precisely the conditions in the Singapore Experiment.

(C) THE INCUBATOR OF INNOVATION IS THE OFTEN POWERLESS, CASH-STRAPPED PRIMARY GROUP OF CROSS-DISCIPLINARY EXPERTS

Richard Branson has touched upon a vital principle. The source of innovation is the primary group, the extended family of people with tacit knowledge of each other's talents and the intimacy to evoke these.[7] This explains why TIP scored so well on the familial dimension in our research. Max Weber called this *gemeinschaft*, a group similar to that which nurtures children, but also nurtures innovation. Here everyone knows everyone, and the culture is full of information and affection.

In direct contrast is *gesellschaft*, otherwise known as a secondary group, with official positions, roles, set tasks, responsibilities and functions. Units of any size above 150 are forced to be secondary groups. Graduate schools at universities, including business schools, are secondary groups. Were the TIP course to be pulled back into the Business School it would become a secondary group subject to the same regulations as other departments. In such groups nearly everything is structured and pre-classified. Behaving in unprecedented ways can upset that structure, can imperil official positions.

Now primary groups are rarely well paid. They are small, even insignificant if one thinks in terms of weight, power and resources. They may exist within larger organizations in the shape of teams. Tom Peters calls them 'skunk groups', which hints at their reputation as less than salubrious, yet it is in such groups that minds mingle, that winning ideas emerge.[8] As a team interacts over time its members become intimate, and a primary-group culture of familiarity emerges.

We are now beginning to understand why the TIP course was so enjoyable for members and why it led to forty-six innovative start-ups from the English-speaking class alone. Not only was it an extended family and primary group, but 50 per cent of the time was given over to team-work in groups of six and seven. Moreover its duration of four months was long enough to extract from fellow programme members much of their information and talent. Attempts to stay close together for longer periods may risk repetition and failing to talk to others beyond the group.

We can also grasp the wisdom of Harvard's new campus, which is to build protective walls around the cross-disciplinary primary group, which has self-organized around a shared achievement fantasy of the future. These project groups could be amazingly inventive and, with the Charles River symbolically between them and the graduate schools they came from, their autonomy is assured. Instead of being just 'pushed' by their disciplines they are in addition 'pulled' by their vision of what might be achieved through novel combinations. They would be paid by results, attracting more and more funds as their records proved innovative.

(D) SCHOOLS OF BUSINESS MAY NOT BE THE
INSTITUTIONS BEST SUITED FOR PROMOTING
INNOVATION

The tension between the Nanyang Technopreneurship Center and the Business School at NTU about who should now 'own' technopreneurship is a fascinating glimpse into the trials of innovation. The vision of the TIP course is to help the entire campus, including every graduate school and every department therein, find its way to commercial application. Innovators are not mainly motivated by money, as we have seen. What innovators want is to see something they have discovered or created change the lives of many people for the better.

That graduate schools in a university, or inter-disciplinary primary groups created from these, should approach the markets by way of a business school bureaucracy is not necessarily desirable. Business schools including Harvard, Nanyang and the Judge Business School at Cambridge may do their job well, but what is that job? It is to serve large corporations from which comes most of their sponsorship. Business schools even mimic the departments of large corporations with departments of Marketing, Production, Finance and Control, Human Resources, Strategy and International Relations. In any start-up or small innovative organization that remains a primary group, this division of labour has not yet taken root. Experts in, say, human resources are not necessary in a start-up because relations are spontaneous and informal. When the corporation grows to hundreds and thousands then the specialists, which business schools educate, become necessary.

It follows that entrepreneurship and primary-group activity does not challenge most business school departments, nor develop their careers and expertise. From their point of view a start-up is primitive, an acorn, not an oak. Almost inevitably entrepreneurship becomes a poor relation to other departments, taught by persons who have never specialized. Entrepreneurs are mostly too poor in their early ventures to donate money to business schools and once they grow big they need specialist help, not a re-telling of their past glory.

On top of this is the question of whether MBAs, which are the chief product of most business schools, have much desire to become entrepreneurs. Part of the purpose of business schools is to inject students into corporations half-way to the top, rather than making them start at the bottom, as must entrepreneurs. An MBA would be sorely disappointed if offered a contingent salary and a 10 per cent chance of the company surviving, which is what entrepreneurs must face.

Indeed the more successful a business school, the greater the loss of earnings a graduate entrepreneur would have to face. We recently interviewed Professor Clayton Christiansen,[9] the Harvard Business School's resident expert on innovation. He told us (before the recent crunch) that an MBA graduating in 2008 could expect a starting salary of $150,000 plus a sign-on bonus of a roughly equal amount. Who would turn down a starting salary of $300,000 and exchange this for the kind of hazards and poverty an entrepreneur must cope with? This would be done only by a person who had something of far greater importance than profit maximization in mind, an idea in which s/he passionately believed.

Not surprisingly, then, start-up companies and entrepreneurs do not recruit MBAs from Harvard in any appreciable numbers, although Rte 128 is only a few miles distant. Silicon Valley does not recruit from among Stanford University MBAs to any noticeable degree. Entrepreneurial 'tecchies' tend to go straight to venture capitalists with their ideas and do not usually employ business-school types. The same is true around Cambridge University, where a cluster of high-tech businesses in the fens around Cambridge is called 'the Cambridge Phenomenon'. To my knowledge they do not recruit MBAs from the Judge Business School. They could not afford to and there seems scant interest on either side.

The JBS actually includes an entrepreneurship department, directed by Professor Shai Vyakarnam, a native of India, who gives a much-admired course in a building separate from JBS, which as many as 140 post-graduate students attend. What is significant is that only 25 of these, around 16 per cent, come from the Judge Business School itself. The rest are chemists, biologists, physicists, engineers and members of the entire gamut of graduate programmes at the university.[10] Surely such statistics reveal that innovation and entrepreneurship are not principally business specialities, but an opportunity for any creative person in any of several disciplines to benefit fellow beings?

No wonder that NTC not only avoided NTU Business School but also the business school at the University of Washington in its travels to the USA. The ideal target was the Bioengineering Department there, full of people with discoveries they wanted to commercialize and ideas they sought to realize. NTC's mission is to serve the whole of Nanyang Technological University, not to be a sub-specialty of business. Innovation is something wider and more fundamental than business. This is something those designing the Allston campus seem to have understood, that inter-disciplinary primary groups have direct access to markets, unmediated by business specialists unless such are requested.

So far from thinking first and foremost about a lot of money for the individual entrepreneur, Tan Teng-Kee's course focuses on altruism rather than egotism. Entrepreneurs will be fulfilled not by what they get but by what they give to others. That the programme begins and ends at the Chinese Heritage Centre on campus is an important part of this theme. Just as NTU is the gift of Chinese immigrant entrepreneurs, so participants in the programme must pass this gift on to others. If they make money from their enterprise, what better way to spend it than to endow education?

The secret of the rise of the Chinese diaspora and now the rise of the PRC is that economic development, innovation especially, is treated as a branch of learning, as a heritage to be passed down the generations. The Chinese tend to avoid the stomach-expanding advertised products so admired in the West: McDonald's, Kentucky Fried Chicken, Dunkin' Donuts, Alka Seltzer to make sure all these stay down, and potato chips. Only Anglo-American economic orthodoxy regards one million dollars' worth of potato chips as equal to one million dollars' worth of microchips. East Asians know better, distinguishing price from value. It is microchips that help educate the culture: they are the 'rice of industry' itself, the brains in a thousand different products.

We may conclude that business schools as we know them are not in the forefront of innovation and are economically tied to the already powerful and wealthy who find it chronically difficult to renew themselves. Innovators are very much underdogs, who merit all the respect and caring we can lavish on them, an issue to which we now turn.

(E) INNOVATORS ARE THE LAST MINORITY
TO BE FULLY EMANCIPATED

For centuries we have been trying to emancipate minorities. First, it was people without property, then women, then Black Americans, then 'illegal' immigrants working but not receiving benefits. But there is one minority which is always in trouble, all the more so because their difference from the rest of us is voluntary and resembles acts of seeming defiance. This is the creative minority. Many regard such persons as subversive, 'UnAmerican', traitors to the social order, who dare to take exception to the status quo and offer something new.

These two ways of being different, involuntary difference and chosen difference, sometimes overlap. Hence someone born of a Nonconformist or Quaker family who knew he was perforce different was likely to act differently as well. There was little to lose. A vast amount of our entrepreneurship comes from immigrants, people who decided to act as they felt themselves to be, different from the rest of us. Britain's 7% to 8% of Nonconformists produced 50% of its entrepreneurs, as we saw earlier. We owe a real debt of gratitude to those with the courage to act and think differently, who use their education not as an escalator to a higher rung on the corporate ladder, but as an opportunity to reconcile dilemmas.

Given our concepts of economic rationality and profit maximization, who would deliberately defy odds of around 9 to 1 in an attempt to realize an ideal? Only a very exceptional person who cared a lot more for their ambitious goal than for money would take such a risk. So, far from such persons being fat-cats and millionaires, they are perhaps the most selfless among us. Of course, some become rich and subsequently join political parties who protect their money. McClelland found it was the children of entrepreneurs who turned conservative;[11] however, were we to catch innovators at the moment of their innovation, we might find them to be the most deserving minority of all time.

A national culture that takes innovation seriously has to locate such persons and nurture them, because without our help these primary groups of excited dreamers are very vulnerable to exploitation. The fact that they care so much for their ideals leaves others free to exploit the reality of the profits generated. But we short-change these people at our peril. They are our culture's most valuable resource. Indeed there is mounting evidence that we should treat them like no other students and that lavish generosity to them pays off in spades. If we look at all the people who volunteer to help TIP students for nothing – the venture capitalists, the mentors, the entrepreneurs who went before them, the innovative companies that open their doors, the fourteen-hour days worked by Tan Teng-Kee, the free work by alumni, the nominal fees paid to instructors and the multitasking of all concerned – then the ratio of teachers to learners is almost 1 to 1, much of the help given free.

Shai Vyakarnam at the Judge Business School reckons that he has twice the number of teachers compared to learners. There are 140 students and nearly 300 volunteers. He rarely mentions his connection with the Judge Business School lest volunteers hesitate to donate their time to an institution already well off. Rather he emphasizes the aspiring young people from all corners of the university who seek to learn. The reason he needs so many volunteers is that students split up into groups according to their backgrounds, so that electronic engineers counsel persons in that field, even as bio-medical students convene around an entrepreneur in that area. He is personally touched by the number of people willing to give their time to his classes and nurture creativity.

What the Singapore Experiment and the vision of Harvard's Allston Campus teach us is that developing innovators and technopreneurs is above all a labour of love and devotion. Just as these innovators are dedicated to their dreams, so those assisting them need to be dedicated to would-be innovators, indeed a whole ecosystem of stimulating friendships and networked engagements is necessary. The bottle-neck has never been in the number of persons willing to aspire, but in the number of persons willing to listen, critique, encourage and nurture aspirations. Cultures typically produce what they most admire. It is in the soil of our admiration that innovators grow.

11 What are the implications of being able to teach innovation?

This chapter will very briefly describe some of the world's most pressing problems and argue that these can only be solved by eliciting a wave of innovation among new generations. Innovation is not simply required to tackle these specific problems one by one – it is required for an ethical culture capable of generating innovative solutions. I shall examine the character of innovative persons and pedagogies as described in this research and ask if we can afford to do without these. Is the teaching of innovation a form of moral teaching? Is the innovative society the good society?

But let us first deal with the pressing problems confronting us. We may have seriously altered our climate through industrial pollution, a possibility that could test our ingenuity to its limits. The rise of India and China threatens to send the price of many commodities skyhigh. Were emerging countries to imitate the energy usage of the USA then their far denser populations would not have enough breathable air or clean water to survive. Their energy saving must be much more elaborate just to avoid catastrophe. We currently drive cars so large and heavy that 80 per cent of the energy is used in moving the vehicle itself and only 20 per cent is expended on moving its occupants.[1] In turn, this necessitates millions of tons of heat-reflecting tarmac. One consequence of our addiction is that oil supplies are so scarce that we have started to fight over these, a process that drives up the price, since oil comes from some of the world's most unstable regions. Speculation is rife. So desperate are various nations to secure the scarce resources necessary for industrial development that some of the most despicable regimes in the world are propped up by their energy customers, who collude in widespread persecution and oppression. 'Black gold' makes ruthless rivals of us all.

AIDS now affects almost a quarter of the population in much of Africa, where millions subsist on less than a dollar a day, unable to afford either medicine or proper nutrition. This almost certainly eliminates the chances of economic take-off and may be only the first of several pandemics sweeping through populations whose immune systems are weakened by malnutrition. Middle-class medicines developed in affluent nations are unaffordable and not available in the quantities likely to be needed. Among the wretched of the earth are a sizeable proportion of Muslims and the very real danger is that the widening gap between rich and poor could mutate into the clash of civilizations featured in the work of Samuel P. Huntington,[2] that the growing inequality in the world drives many of those deemed inferior into a suicidal rage. Can democracy survive the willingness of just a few people willing to commit suicide in the midst of us? What can deter people eager to die provided they force us to accompany them? It might be thought that such horrendous problems are beyond even the most innovative problem-solvers, but surely we should try?

So what characterizes the learning of innovative persons as revealed in this book? What ecosystems and pedagogies enlighten them? Suppose millions of us could be educated to be more innovative, what might this do for the cultural characteristics of a nation? I shall briefly consider the following:

(a) The courage to confront world problems
(b) The widest possible tolerance for diversity encountered in relationships of equality
(c) A capacity to mediate, reconcile and construct larger meanings
(d) The transcendence of scarcity
(e) An infinite not a finite game
(f) Eras of creativity – often shadowed by backlash
(g) Substituting 'soft' for 'hard' power
(h) The survival of the 'fittingest' and most harmonious

(i) An economy based on knowledge and complexity

(j) Innovation as an ethical culture

(A) THE COURAGE TO CONFRONT WORLD PROBLEMS

One characteristic of innovative learning is its critical attitudes to the status quo.[3] If learners do not see a flaw in present practices, they will search hard until they find one. It is no use to come up with something new if existing products suffice; hence the entrepreneur and innovator is in a restless search for 'pain points', problems with the present system that cry out for a remedy.[4]

It follows that the crises described earlier would whet the appetites of genuine innovators. Many of our problems revolve around the polluting effects of oil and its volatile price. It follows that replacing oil with renewable sources of energy like wind power, solar power, thermal power, wave power and hydrogen might halt fighting in the Middle East, Georgia, Sudan, Nigeria etc., and rescue nations from a desperate scarcity that breeds enmity and power politics. The carbon footprint is not just polluting the planet, it is highly combustible and foments war. Another avenue to remedy is the replacement of the internal combustion engine, a great challenge to innovators. Do we need heavy steel cars driven on roads of tarmac thick enough to take their weight? Why worship machine efficiency when the key to our survival is resource efficiency? Why not cars of plastic and fibreglass, designed to customers' specifications in local workshops? Of course, the problems and barriers are many. It has always been so, but what a challenge to our imaginations!

Necessity is the mother of invention, and the Indian pharmaceutical industry has been showing us the way. With its 300 million impoverished people, the Indian industry faces the problem of stopping pandemics amongst its poorest. A composite AIDS tablet, containing a cocktail of different remedies and impossibly expensive in the West, is now helping the under-developed world to withstand this deadly siege. We need all our wits about us to withstand such crises.

(B) THE WIDEST POSSIBLE TOLERANCE FOR DIVERSITY ENCOUNTERED IN RELATIONSHIPS OF EQUALITY

Innovative people find it very difficult to function without including in their world view every person, every animal, every idea, phenomenon or possibility. Since creativity involves the combination of two or more elements previously remote from each other and in different realms of discourse, all barriers need to be crossed, all cultures explored and all relevant disciplines understood. But it is not enough to descend on South America like the conquistadores and put the natives to the sword. Colonial relationships intent on exploiting natural resources are sterile. You can only understand the mental constructs of strangers in relationships of equality. You will not succeed in connecting two important ideas if you regard one as inferior. Equality is a norm designed to elicit from the other something important to you which that person knows. If the other's perspective is not taken very seriously you cannot benefit from discovering it.

No wonder then that students in 'technopreneurship' courses at NTC come from more than twenty nations and include Muslims, Christians, Buddhists, Jews, Hindus and Confucians. As we shall see in Chapter 12, the more innovative parts of the USA are also the more tolerant and cosmopolitan, accepting gay life-styles and advocating equal opportunities for women and minorities.[5] An innovative course taught by this author at Sungkyunkwan University in South Korea had thirty-five national cultures in attendance. It is not that women or gays necessarily play a vital part in innovative activities, although that is always a possibility, it is simply the habit of letting into your mind ideas or preferences that might be relevant to solving the problem at hand. These might derive from unlikely sources, and if you censor these you limit your own scope.

(C) A CAPACITY TO MEDIATE, RECONCILE AND CONSTRUCT LARGER MEANINGS

Those who put together an innovative combination of resources have to do more than 'tolerate' those resources and treat those who supply them as equals: they need to mediate among contexts of information and reconcile them into a coherent whole. This entails developing larger meanings, not analysing things to pieces, but constructing and designing whole systems. It begins in dialogue but ends in a more encompassing synthesis than you had before. We have already seen through our research that our subjects reconciled and fused intellectuality with emotion, absorbing information with thinking and choosing for oneself, competitiveness with familial support, playing with seriousness and so on. The process of fusing these contrasting values is what we mean by human integrity, a set of interacting values attached to one another by moral force and refusing to be divided or split off, a tenacious wholeness from which we derive the word 'holy'. Hence to be innovative you have to have integrity at least as broad as the challenge facing you.

(D) THE TRANSCENDENCE OF SCARCITY

Scarcity is a concept essential to economics. Indeed it is the corner-stone of that discipline that human wants are infinite, but money and resources scarce. Yet economists have always been uneasy with inno-vation, preferring to quote Schumpeter, that innovation is 'a gale of creative destruction' and leave it at that.

They are wise to be wary because innovation removes the cornerstone on which their edifice is built. Of course, money is inher-ently scarce, but ideas, knowledge, visions and embryo creations are unlimited. If I offer you a banana for cash, I can have either the cash or the banana but not both. But if I offer you knowledge for cash, then I get the cash and I keep the knowledge which is now shared between us. The scarcity is gone. Something crucial happens when an economy is based on knowledge-sharing. It was Romeo who said to Juliet, 'the more I give to thee, the more I have', but this does not only apply to love relations, but to two persons or a team who put their heads together and generate more knowledge than they had initially and individually. It is also the everyday experience of the good teacher.

Knowledge not shared but deployed as a weapon of personal advantage against others is sterile. But knowledge shared and synthesized into a broadened perspective expands the minds of all parties to an interaction. Yet the catalyst of creativity must be there, the innovative spark that turns 2+2 into 5 or even 500 (what is silicon worth outside a chip?). Novel combinations have a synergistic quality, an infinitely greater value. If we can remove the notion of scarcity from our working relationships, amazing things may happen. One reason that private enterprise excites us more than the work of government is that people can put their ideas and their resources together and discover they have created surplus value from this. They have more than they started with. This can be a deeply moving and exciting experience.[6]

(E) AN INFINITE NOT A FINITE GAME

It can be useful to see business as a kind of sport or game played within a set of rules. You 'win' such games by out-competing the other team and eliminating it from the contest. In time you may be able to acquire its managers and employees and mobilize these more effectively than before, in which case the larger economy may benefit by players performing better under superior coaching. But of course these are finite games, a series of short, sharp contests in which one company wins and another loses and what one company gains the other loses or surrenders in a climate of enduring scarcity. James P. Carse has contrasted the Finite with the Infinite game.[7] Here are his contrasts.

The Finite Game	The Infinite Game
The purpose is to win	The purpose is to improve the game
Improves through the fittest surviving	Improves through the game evolving
Winners exclude losers	Winners teach losers better plays
Winner takes all	Winnings widely shared
Aims are identical	Aims are diverse
Relatively simple contest	Relatively complex combinations
Rules fixed in advance	Rules changed by agreement
Rules resemble a debating contest	Rules resemble grammar of original utterances

The Finite Game is not wrong. This *is* how many businesses compete. The question is whether it is good enough and whether East Asians, at least in part, have started to play an infinite game which is more innovative, more educational and more suited to the wealth of innovation that societies are now generating. Why not join finite games together into one endless game? Winning is only part of the purpose. The larger purpose is to improve the practice of the game itself through observing what winners do. Rather than the fittest within the game surviving, might not the whole game be evolving to new levels of innovation and excellence?

Is it necessary to exclude losers, to account them failures? Entrepreneurs rise phoenix-like from repeated failures because they learn to play better. They are playing infinitely if they can find enough courage to persist. If we share winnings along with information and opportunities, might we not do better in the end? The scarcity endemic in the Finite Game comes from the fact that everyone's aims are identical. They all want 'goals' or more dollars, or straight As. They want to take away credit from their rivals, but the wonderful family-type atmosphere in the Singapore Experiment comes from aims being diverse and enjoying the sheer variety of different aims that subtract not at all from each other. Here is abundance.

The Finite Game is simple. You win or lose and are seen to do this, often before an audience of adoring fans. But the Infinite Game is subtle and complex, not really a spectator sport but a co-creation of something more complex still, something that joins together all the reasons for past victories. In finite games the rules are fixed in advance and the referee blows his whistle penalizing either team of players. In infinite games the rules are there to be modified and improved upon to give added value to all concerned. Finite games are like debating contests. Someone adds up 'the points' made by each side. The Infinite Game is like the rules of grammatical utterances, allowing you to create what you will within those rules, whose purpose is the clear articulation of ideas. With innovation we find ourselves forever improving and evolving infinite games and teaching each other about this, as we share what we know and pursue diverse objectives. The rules are ours to legislate and re-make so long as we can agree and delight each other with original products and systems.

(F) ERAS OF CREATIVITY – OFTEN SHADOWED BY BACKLASH

The history of mankind has experienced several 'golden ages' that arose as suddenly as they disappeared. We have already enumerated this list but have not dwelt enough on its transience. The amazing rise of China, still a Communist country and very soon to out-perform the rise of Japan a few decades earlier, is simply the latest. But we should not romanticize such periods. They were and too often are shadowed by backlash. The Golden Age of Athens ended in plague and military defeat. The Tang dynasty ended with the widespread massacre of foreigners. Savonarola persuaded even Michelangelo to throw his paintings on the bonfire of vanities. Diversity and its widespread tolerance, even the emergence of new artefacts, makes populations profoundly anxious and neighbouring nations profoundly envious and covetous. The backlash is never far away. The creative minority is too vulnerable and trusting, too welcoming of disorder and ferment.

What is common to all these eras is that masters of their craft knew and admired each other and that sponsors like the Medici family, critics and appreciative audiences were simultaneously present. For a few precious years small groups of people generated an abundance of beauty and mutual stimulation and then it was gone. We must somehow try to make such states more permanent, more lasting. Knowledge suddenly shared and enjoyed in its abundance must be more than vanished episodes in our history.[8]

(G) SUBSTITUTING 'SOFT' FOR 'HARD' POWER

It was Francis Bacon who observed that 'Knowledge is Power'.[9] By this he meant 'hard' power, the ability to make Nature obey us rather than our being at the mercy of the elements, tossed on oceans, crushed in landslides, emaciated by hunger, parched by drought, burnt in fires and devastated by storms. Today we have so much hard power that the boot is on the other foot, the earth is in danger of being damaged by *us*. America under Bush has reverted to 'hard' power in its refusal to endorse the Kyoto Agreement and in its doctrine of pre-emptive wars in Iraq, Afghanistan and elsewhere.

The Harvard political scientist Joseph Nye has written on the subject of knowledge as 'soft power',[10] the power to enlighten, teach, advise, facilitate, create and innovate; not so much power *over* people, but power *through* people, to use Bertrand Russell's distinction. At the height of its influence in the late twentieth century, the USA was the world's prime exponent of soft power, teaching hundreds of thousands of foreign students and turning its universities into cosmopolitan enclaves of diversity and innovation. Alas, this era has passed, enrolments are in decline and most students have moved to other sources of influence, see *The Flight of the Creative Class* by Richard Florida.[11] Even as 'hard power' increased, 'soft power' began to wane. Innovation and the teaching of innovation is clearly the most ambitious and exciting exercise in soft power and in mutual enrichment through shared and abundant knowledge.

(H) THE SURVIVAL OF THE 'FITTINGEST' AND MOST HARMONIOUS

Darwin's theory of evolution had much to say about the 'survival of the fittest'. The vision was of one animal pitted against another in a natural environment, red in tooth and claw, where the fiercest predator survived, a view promoted by Richard Dawkins.[12] But this view is only a small part of reality. Fierce predators are relatively scarce, much as we seem to enjoy them. Darwin was very much a Victorian, more comfortable with imperial conquest than with sexuality. He only grudgingly admitted that part of evolution was bonding with the opposite sex and prodigious rates of reproduction among the more attractive. We animals actually survive by fitting successfully into one another and into environmental niches, like the koala bear clinging to the high, waving branches of the eucalyptus tree.

Indeed, it is a fallacy to see animals themselves as units of survival. What survives is the animal plus its environment or habitat, without which the creature would perish. Nature probably has more co-evolutionary ways of cooperating among species than it has terrible lizards on the prowl, but what ultimately matters is not the survival of the fittest to fight or to run away, but the survival of the fittingest, the animal that fits most effectively and harmoniously into its part of the environment.[13] Many of these adaptations are brilliantly 'innovative', the products of millions of evolutionary trials, perpetuated by success.

Innovation is among other things a state of harmonious combination, not just between ideas and resources, but between suppliers and partners, suppliers and customers, opportunities and ventures. Successful products become part of the environment, aspects of living systems that sustain us and magnets for other products that enhance those systems. One of the inestimable economic advantages of Chinese and Japanese culture is that wā, harmony in Japanese, and *Zhong he*, harmony in Chinese, and *guanxi*, sustaining relationships, are among its greatest business virtues,[14] while the West seems more enthralled by the Tyrannosaurus rex or the Great White Shark's appetite for teenagers. Lao Tzu praised water as a symbol of flexibility, and the wave-forms and the water logic in the reconciliation zones of our research grids and cubes are no coincidence. The Chinese business writer Chin Ning-Chu explains: 'In Asian cultures there is no division between business, spirituality, personal relationships and the art of war. Every aspect of life is interconnected.'[15] Though it is true that innovation has destructive effects and new products make old ones obsolescent, the search is then on for co-creation with other companies, for more sustaining, harmonious, fitting and innovative relationships. This seems to be of particular interest to Asian business writers.[16]

(I) AN ECONOMY BASED ON KNOWLEDGE
AND COMPLEXITY

While we have seen that the synthesis of knowledge with knowledge and mind with mind transcends scarcity and generates wealth, once a product is made and offered on the market it at once becomes more or less scarce. Innovation is the principal way of making products scarce. If, in addition, it is complex and requires rare knowledge to make, that scarcity will last until the patent expires or the same value is generated by different means. Competitors will be racing after you to offer substitutes. Yet for at least a time you will be basking in 'blue ocean strategy', an exploratory environment with few if any competitors.[17]

For all these reasons, knowledge intensity, complexity and innovation together contribute to scarcity and scarcity enhances value. Singapore, China and much of East Asia are in relentless pursuit of products and systems packed with as much knowledge as possible, which educates consumers, users, suppliers, retailers etc. We need to see the Singapore Experiment in its cultural context and this context consists of always trying to render Singaporeans more knowledgeable, intelligent and complex than before and using the economy for its educational potential. Europe and America have been curiously slow to grasp the learning dynamic within economic development. When the Welsh Development Authority sent this author to Korea to solicit the building of factories in Wales, the purpose was to gain manufacturing jobs. No one was concerned with the quality or complexity of these jobs.

In truth every company is an Inquiring System, every new product offered customers is a hypothesis, every decision to buy or not to buy confirms or refutes that hypothesis, and the faster the company fits itself closely into its environment the sooner and better it will learn. Complexity, knowledge intensity and innovation are connected. On the leading edge of knowledge there are more opportunities and fewer competitors than anywhere else. Knowledge tends to branch outwards like the trunk, branches and twigs of a tree, a very popular metaphor in Japan.[18]

To get in among the sprouting twigs is to encounter a score of opportunities for new connections. It is to produce that knowledge yourself and know more about new generations of your product than anyone else. Once a corporation starts to generate knowledge for itself, its lead may be unassailable. What is at stake here is a new vision of world order as a giant knowledge tree, simple at its trunk and roots but ever more complex at its higher branches. Whole nations are now scrambling up that tree, not just its universities but clusters of companies, some of these around its universities. Those high up on the tree can help those below by running down their own simpler work and buying mass manufactures from poorer, less educated countries, thereby hauling those up behind them. Because of the scarcity of new, complex products, developed nations earn good returns on their education and plough the money back into learning. Are Singapore, the Intelligent Island, and its experiments harbingers of this new order?

(J) INNOVATION AS AN ETHICAL CULTURE – A SUMMARY

What innovation requires is nothing less than an ethical culture, a way of listening to and treating fellow innovators that elicits the potential within them. We have seen in this chapter that innovators actively seek problems to solve and are aroused and galvanized by world crises. The history of innovation is through challenge and response. The Singapore Experiment itself was an answer to a challenge. The country's record of entrepreneurship was not good enough.

Innovation requires such a wide diversity of interest and curiosity that we must tolerate everything that is not actively dangerous to us, every race, every people, every idea, every winding path of knowledge and experience. The richer our choices, the more likely we are to discover rare and valuable combinations. All great ages of innovation were cosmopolitan and diverse. And we must approach these contrasting points of view in the spirit of equality or we cannot properly internalize them.

But we must do more than tolerate, we must reconcile, discovering the common threads of humanity within the strangest of people. The several points of view need not simply to be respected but designed into a larger whole. This is what the participants in the two programmes learned to do, fusing highly contrasting values with each other so that their pedagogy was not just realistic but idealistic as well.

What gives such a culture its joyfulness and delight is that, however briefly, scarcity has been transcended: knowledge shared becomes knowledge expanded and people see themselves as the origins of new meanings and new satisfactions. That these make money allows the process to continue on a larger scale. We find personal fulfilment in making our visions come true and in organizing knowledge around ourselves. This essentially constitutes a 'game' that goes on for ever, an infinite game. This comes naturally to those nations who see economic development as a form or relational learning within the whole community. If we join a whole series of win/lose finite contests together, the larger meaning will emerge from these and we will create more effective plays with more effective rules on which we have agreed. Are there perhaps 'rules of innovation' itself?

On rare occasions the earth's peoples have witnessed brief eras of intense innovation and creativity, yet these eras balance on a knife-edge, besieged by people made anxious by the diversity, by the tolerance and by the seeming chaos. A key to understanding may lie in the concept of soft power, the power to illuminate, entertain, educate and elicit innovation in others, so that a microcosm of the world's most enterprising people beat a path to your door, attracted by the spirit of discovery. The secret of such cultures is the survival of the fittingest, those best able to form close, symbiotic relationships with the wider culture, characterized by the ideals of harmony.

Such an economy puts the ability to learn, faster than rivals, at the apex of its value system. Economic development is a race to climb a knowledge tree and innovate among its highest branches and twigs. Modern enterprise generates knowledge rooted in higher learning. A nation developing such an ethic will find that many of its former troubles go into spontaneous remission. Who would choose to be high on drugs if they could be high on ideas and possibilities? Who would choose to exploit people if they knew how to satisfy them? Who would choose to hog the world's resources if they could generate these? Innovative ecosystems are frail qualities of culture, which we are just beginning to understand.

12 Is a new creative class arising?

The evidence suggests that the Singapore Experiment is not an isolated example. Richard Florida, a geographer, and several other writers have suggested that what might be happening is nothing less than a world-wide phenomenon he calls *The Rise of the Creative Class*.[1] If such a class is arising not just in America, but in Europe and East Asia, then what is set out in this book may be an effective way of teaching a new class of innovators and creative employees. This research might be even more widely relevant.

Florida began by imagining a time traveller who had switched from 1900 to 1950 and again from 1950 to 2000 and beyond. At first blush the half-century to 1950 contained most of the world-changing surprises, the automobile, the Federal Highway System, the aeroplane and jet engine, the airline industry, radio and television, the telephone and even the first computer. The world of 1900 would be barely recognizable from the heights of Manhattan skyscrapers.

Yet the time traveller from 1950 to 2000 would recognize most, if not all, of our technologies. Admittedly, computers have become personal and telephones mobile and we are now connected to the Internet, but the general principles were not so far apart. Our traveller to 2000 would not be whisked out of his horse and buggy and brownstone into a totally transformed world. He would surely be less bewildered. Perhaps this is so, but our traveller could be bewildered for different reasons. What changed in the first part of the century was the physical infrastructure. What changed in the second half of the century were norms, values and life-styles. Florida comments:

> At work he would find a new dress code and schedule and new rules. He would see office workers dressed like folks relaxing at the weekend in jeans and open neck shirts and be shocked to learn that

these occupy positions of authority. People at the office would seemingly come and go as they pleased. Women and non-whites would be managers. Individuality and non-conformity would be valued over conformity to organizational norms ... [but] His ethnic jokes would fall embarrassingly flat. His smoking would get him banished from the parking lot and his two-martini lunch would raise genuine concern. There would be mixed race couples and same sex couples. What happened to the Ladies Clubs, Moose Lodges and bowling leagues?[2]

Florida admits that the creative 'class' is an unusual one. For one thing it lacks class-consciousness and seems unaware of its own existence. It has not even begun to mobilize socio-political muscle and may be too pre-occupied with creating to do so. It is not a concerted movement at all. Nevertheless, it constitutes a formidable competitive advantage for the regions it occupies and for the nation. By fusing science and art, whole new industries are being created, e.g. computer graphics, digital film and music, liquid-crystal display and animation. I shall consider Florida's evidence for a new creative class under the following heads:

(a) The clustered characteristics of a creative class
(b) The economic and geographical background
(c) The dominant value system
(d) The preferred workplace
(e) 'If you can fill each unforgiving minute ...'
(f) The consuming of experiences
(g) The fusion of social and cultural movements
(h) Is this class now in flight from America?

(A) THE CLUSTERED CHARACTERISTICS
OF A CREATIVE CLASS

Creative persons have always clustered and they do so today in key parts of the USA, Europe and Asia. They clustered, albeit fleetingly, in Athens, Rome, the Florence of the Medici, Silicon Valley, Route 128 around Boston and so on. They share the culture of a particular region and this region takes off. Today there are creative clusters in America around San Francisco; Seattle; Boston-Cambridge; Austin, Texas; Boulder, Colorado; Greater New York; Los Angeles; and Portland, Oregon, to name a few. There are around 40 million members of America's creative class and they are densely packed in just a few urban regions. Between 15 and 20 per cent of these dense urban environments create more than 80 per cent of America's innovative output. Florida posits a 'super creative core' which is much less than 40 million, but around these group creative professionals who facilitate their activities: agents, publishers, venture capitalists and intellectual property lawyers.

This is more than post-industrialism, more than the service economy which is often low paid, more than the knowledge economy or the symbolic analysts identified by Robert Reich.[3] The creative class deals with new combinations of sometimes old ideas and produces innovative outcomes. Florida is a geographer who classifies employed persons by the work they do. By his reckoning the creative class stood at 3 million in 1980, had increased to 30 million by 2000 and is nearly 40 million today, despite a severe drain of foreigners during the Bush years which witnessed hostility to minority persuasions in general. The creative class earns over twice as much per head as the service class and the manufacturing class. Its numbers, its influence and its income are rising.[4] It is also the norm-setting class, leading fashion rather than following it, modelling new aspirations, careers, trends and life-styles. Florida points out that 'Artists, musicians, professors and scientists have always set their own hours, dressed in relaxed and casual clothes and worked in stimulating environments.' While the 'no collar' workplace certainly appears more casual than the old, it replaces traditional, hierarchical systems of control with new forms of self-management, peer recognition and pressure, and intrinsic forms of motivation. This class does have authorities to obey, but these are the authorities of science, of the problems that need solving, of the super-ordinate goals to which they have committed themselves and around which they cluster.[5]

(B) THE ECONOMIC AND GEOGRAPHICAL BACKGROUND

Innovation within the creative class takes the form of cross-connecting ideas thrown up at the leading edges of several disciplines. The key to innovation is 'better recipes not just more cooking', to quote Paul Romer.[6] The knowledge typically comes from nearby universities, but the cross-connecting is done by thousands of start-up companies in the vicinity. Einstein referred to the process as 'combinatory play', which was both serious and playful. This 'destroys one's gestalt in favour of a better one'. Florida quotes Joel Mokyr: 'Economists and historians alike realize that there is a deep difference between *homo economicus* and *homo creativus*. One makes the most of what nature permits him to have, the other rebels against nature's dictates. Technological creativity, like all creativity is an act of rebellion.'[7] As such it is frail, often provocative and all too easily arrested.

Wealth originates not in patents, recipes or formulae but in the people who make these. Unlike other resources good ideas generate a law of increasing returns. Creativity seems to be the product of the hurly-burly life of the street, of spontaneous interactions, accidental meetings and stimulating mutuality. This was described by Jane Jacobs in *The Death and Life of Great American Cities*, of which Greenwich Village was an example.[8] Florida notes: 'What really drove the boom of the nineties in America was not greed or even rampant venture capitalism and high-tech entrepreneurship but a tremendous unleashing of creativity.'[9]

We are facing an explosion in the pace and intensity of these forms. The more information there is the more are the potential connections among these and this process is probably exponential. The creative sector of the economy accounts for most of the wealth creation in North America and Western Europe. Its 39 million employees, roughly 30% of the total, produce 47% of the wealth in the USA, 2 trillion dollars. In contrast the service sector with 56 million employees, 44% of the total, produces only 30% of the wealth, or 1.3 trillion dollars. Frank Levy and Richard Murname have looked at the kind of jobs increasing fastest from a low ebb just a few years ago. They highlight expert thinking, complex communication, cognitive tasks and non-routine manual work.[10] If we look at salary gains in the last two decades, the creative class has prospered and the service, manufacturing and agricultural classes have languished.

Economic development also correlates significantly with literacy, the ability to speak and write using your own combinational skills. A 1% rise in the literacy league tables of nations accompanies a 2.5% rise in labour productivity and a 1.5% rise in GDP per capita.[11] There is also a strong correlation between innovative high-tech regions and Florida's Gays Toleration Index. The point is not that gay people are disproportionately innovative, for of this there is no evidence. It is rather that tolerance of this group is generalized to all interests and lifestyles, and being gay is among these.[12]

(C) THE DOMINANT VALUE SYSTEM

Of special interest to us are the values of the creative class. These include strong individuality and meritocracy, with a preference for the competent over the wealthy and with openness to diversity, since merit has to be searched for in a wide arc of interests and preferences. This class has a natural sympathy for outsiders, since so many creative people have placed themselves outside by volition. They are characterized by 'egalitarian elitism'. They seek out the most talented persons they can find and employ norms of equality to elicit as much information from such people as possible. Yet they bridge the divides of taste and preference more than class divides. One interviewee described his workplace as looking 'like the United Nations but minus the black faces'.

In interviews the creative class showed themselves to be 'postscarcity', being much more interested in ideas and self-expression than in survival, security, salary or even stock-options. They also actively search for greater responsibility. They wish to be the source of change itself. They work in order to learn, develop themselves and share intense experiences. Their sense of self is immersed in their work and they seek to express this. The desire is for a life with multi-dimensional stimuli. David Brooks in *Bobos in Paradise* claimed these persons had a fusion of 'Bourgeois' and 'Bohemian' values,[13] but Florida's interviews showed that they disliked these labels. They felt that their synthesis had transcended stereotypes. They prefer not to be a type at all and scorn any notion of self-conscious display or conspicuous creativity. They seek to solve problems and make new connections, not to pose before the public in any recognizable stance.

Members of the creative class also have a strong sense of 'place' or location. They have deliberately sought out an urban environment full of variety, a rich cosmopolitan mix. They like to immerse themselves in local activities and live life to the full. They are under-subscribed to the more formalized notions of culture – ballet, symphony and opera – and over-subscribed to cultural activities in which they can immerse themselves, such as the local exhibition, the informal meeting, the ethnic restaurant or dance venue and of course the street scene.

(D) THE PREFERRED WORKPLACE

You can tell a lot about the creative class by how they prefer to work and the kind of employers they choose. In extended surveys of IT workers, Florida and Stolarick[14] found that of eleven factors in the workplace, the degree of challenge led all the rest by wide margins. Challenge was emphasized by 67%, with flexibility of work-style second at 31.4%. Base pay was mentioned by only 25.3%, with benefits last at 9.7%. Florida suggests that what they really want is a reconciliation of the fun, conviviality and artistry of the 'hair salon' and the focus, drive and science of the 'machine shop'. They prefer flexible schedules because they may have other activities and responsibilities and their competence is between their ears and/or stored in a thumb drive around their necks, so they can 'work' in many places and are very mobile.

They prefer open office design and layout where other workers can be seen, with views to the outside which everyone can share. They like communal places to meet and chat and 'hang out', and semi-private corners in which to huddle. They like indirect lighting and abundant art on the walls. The idea is not to chain workers to their desks or ask why they are moving about but to encourage them to make casual contacts between persons in different roles. The most valuable staff members tend to be in the middle of the floor for easier access, rather than being around the peripheries in exclusive corner offices with better views.[15]

There are distinct ways of managing the creative class. Microsoft's rules are an interesting example as was the 'HP Way', now largely abandoned to more structured controls. Management hires smart people willing to think in unusual ways, and throws odd-ball questions at them in interviews. It expects them to fail but to do so in pursuit of innovative aspirations, to correct their mistakes not repeat them and to persevere in attempts to succeed. It seems to maintain the start-up mentality, hence the mythologies around garages and backrooms. The reason for having an office resembling a home is to evoke the primary group, the family-type atmosphere. 'Management by wandering about' originated in the early Hewlett Packard era and saw leaders moving among researchers and bundling their ideas together.[16]

Rather than fitting into pre-defined job descriptions, members of the creative class enrich their jobs and 'sculpt' them into new forms demanded by new challenges. Peter Drucker has described them as de facto volunteers, who do the work they most love for the sake of completing it.[17] They are subject to some controls, but these are 'soft controls', deriving from the science of what they are doing, shared purpose and commitments, promises to peers and the planned convergence of parallel processes.

The old style of employment described by William Whyte in *The Organization Man* saw salaried executives trading their working lives for money, status, security and an identity as an IBM or GM functionary.[18] This has given way to much looser, much more temporary memberships, averaging around three years, where the continuity is

inside the person or teams of persons, not so much inside the corporation. Employees may change their jobs more often than their car pools.
They exchange their ideas and their energies for money to live on but if
not adequately challenged they move on to another company with an
'idiosyncratic deal' that uses them better and more adventurously.

One example of the self-organizing nature of seemingly spontaneous innovation is the Open Source Software Movement, surrounding the activities of Linux, a Finnish start-up, and the now burgeoning
Apache network. Open Source means that the source code by which
the software was programmed is open to the purchaser, as opposed
to the closed-source, proprietary software sold by Microsoft, where
only the use is for sale not the logic. The two systems offer contrasting
emphases on the sheer joys of innovation versus making profits from
its sale. Open Source hugely accelerates information-sharing and
the capacity to mount one innovation on the top of another, with the
ability to customize and transform the code you have purchased. In
contrast, the need to make money from successive closed-source software packages may mean slowing the pace of innovation until the
profits have been harvested.[19] It is an ominous sign for Western economies that the PRC has opted for open-source software, which may
speed up their innovation.

What happens, at least in boom times, is that companies and
cities, including Singapore, compete to attract members of the creative
class. Companies may provide a crèche for children of employees,
benefits for same-gender couples, subsidized healthy foods, free tickets
to local events and amenities that make an office seem like home. This
can have the effect of freeing up their minds for innovative efforts by
taking care of routine chores. In exchange they may work a seven-day
week, take their challenges home and sleep on them.

Given the relentless pace of work it is vital that employees do
not burn out, but find within the workplace sources of renewal and
amenities with which to refresh themselves. Research by Theresa
Amabile at Harvard[20] revealed that deadlines, threats, crises and contrived pressures are all inimical to creativity as are money incentives to

do tasks that in many cases have yet to be defined! Creative employees pace themselves and as John Cleese has pointed out[21] most ideas incubate and pop into one's mind overnight or while resting, so that pressurizing employees is self-defeating, while giving them amenities at work that permit periods of relaxation and recuperation facilitates innovation.

There is an implicit bargain. The company will do more for you if you do more for the company. The company will more resemble home if you spend more time in the company and less at home. The distinction between work and play begins to erode, because playful work is the most fulfilling and sustaining aspect of life. Yet Florida deplores tokenism: the odd ping-pong table or espresso coffee machine will not do the trick. There must be a genuinely innovative environment like that of IDEO close to Stanford University,[22] which consults in design breakthroughs and for whom Susan Tan, Tan Teng-Kee's daughter and herself a TIP graduate, now works.

(E) 'IF YOU CAN FILL EACH UNFORGIVING MINUTE ...'
One sizeable advantage possessed by the creative class is its prodigious capacity for hard work and long hours, with every corner of their lives crowded with events. This may also account for its political weakness. There is no time to organize politically. But when you work smart and smarter you are often unaware of working harder. Solving a problem is deeply satisfying and there is a 'collapse of time' and a 'flow experience' similar to that described by psychologist Mihaly Csikszentmihalyi.[23] We also found students in the TIP course working past midnight and at weekends, almost oblivious to time.

One secret of America's resurgence in the nineties, when many expected Japan to overtake, was that Americans work harder and longer than other nations, especially the creative employees. While much of Europe still regards long hours as a form of exploitation by overly oppressive employers, the USA had broken through the 'pain threshold' to the exhilaration of Olympic-style excellence. It is not blue collar workers who work long hours but members of the creative class who do not want to stop and take home the ferment that is within their minds. US workers as of 2001 worked 137 more hours a year than the Japanese, 260 hours more than British employees and 500 more than Germans. They also worked longer days and took less vacation time. But this was mostly among senior employees, not unionized, hourly workers.[24] The creative class thinks first of the success of their ventures, not whether it is 5.0 p.m. and the end of their contracted hours.

If you want to live creatively time becomes the scarcest and most precious commodity. There may be abundance in other spheres but there is rarely enough time. The talk of 'quality time' with friends, lovers and children testifies to the search, perhaps vain, for instant intimacy. This time must have the highest quality because it is so short. Such is this time shortage that it has been estimated that if Bill Gates drops a $5 bill, it is not worth his time to stoop and pick it up! The responses to the shortage of time are many: multi-tasking, taking work home and bringing the relaxations of home to work, drinking coffee at Starbucks with your computer before you and your mobile phone at your ear, carrying on conversations with the dashboard of your car while driving and parallel processes at work wherein features of a product are worked on simultaneously and then synthesized.

(F) THE CONSUMING OF EXPERIENCES

The creative class consumes fewer things, objects and products than experiences, for which it has a voracious appetite – see the first dimension we measured in Chapter 5. The value of experience is that you become what Alvin Toffler calls a 'prosumer',[25] someone who consumes in order to produce better, like Open Source software, which is internalized then transformed into a new program. Members of this class need to pack their lives with the intense, memorable, multi-dimensional experience of actually doing valued tasks. For such reasons they prefer participation in sports over passively watching them. They enjoy running, swimming, sailing, rock climbing, cycling and swimming, exercise they can do themselves even if not expertly.

Theirs is an imaginative hedonism. Experiences have the advantage that they rarely use up the world's resources and may exist largely in the mind and body. Conspicuous consumption is frowned upon as a distraction. A cabin in the woods furnished by IKEA will suffice. Whereas wealth once meant a heap of possessions, for this class it is the quality of life's experiences.

We find evidence of this in events like the Boston Marathon that expanded from 225 runners when first staged in 1964 to 20,000 today. Similarly Health Club membership has expanded from 15 million in the eighties to more than 30 million today.[26] John Sculley who notoriously fired Steve Jobs from Apple ran five miles a day in the nineties before starting work to compensate for an otherwise sedentary job. Such activity is thought to sharpen you up and relieve stress.

Most of these exercises are less in order to beat other people or compete against them than for the experience of sport for its own sake. Such sports are typically unorganized. People want to set their own rules and go at their own pace. This class are rarely football fans or followers of spectator sports, made ecstatic or violent by victory or defeat. Among the dichotomies they resolve is the Cartesian mind–body dualism. The body is seen as a work of art to be fine-tuned and kept fit. To this end, reports in *Men's Fitness* magazine give a distribution of fitness across America curiously similar to those regions where the creative class reside.[27] Areas with year-round sunshine like San Diego have an obvious advantage, but the pattern of 'fit creativity' remains clear.

(G) THE ORIGINS OF THE CREATIVE CLASS LIE IN THE FUSION OF SOCIAL AND CULTURAL MOVEMENTS

It is important to ask where the creative class sprang from. Carl Gustav Jung spoke of creativity as arising from *coincidentia oppositorum*, the coincidence of once-opposed trends forming a new synthesis.[28] Florida traces the origins of Silicon Valley to the Berkeley Free Speech Movement of 1964, the first major American campus revolt at UC Berkeley and one aimed at the stultifying culture of academic conformity, as opposed to later revolts which were fuelled more by the Vietnam War and Civil Rights protests. The Berkeley revolt was targeted at Free Speech, the right of students to associate on campus and champion causes not on their curricula. That the Bay Area was the first to rebel, largely on learning-style grounds, may not be a coincidence.

Accounts of this and other student and cultural movements come to us mostly via their critics. Daniel Bell, in *The Cultural Contradictions of Capitalism*,[29] argued that an expansion of the production ethos and the 'calculative mode' of traditional business had needed a corresponding consumption ethic, if everything that was produced was to be sold and consumed. Network television had bombarded millions of homes with soft messages of self-indulgence for a decade or more and the ethic of consumption was now so strong that it was devouring the production ethic itself. The result was less a counter-culture than a 'counterfeit' culture of parasitic children from mostly affluent homes flaunting an ethic of 'Peace and Love', by which they meant a life of sensuous experiences which were fashionable and which contradicted the calculative mode at every point. If the straight culture was planned, industrious, artful, deliberate and economizing, then the counter-culture would be the logical opposite, spontaneous, laid back, artless, random and self-indulgent. If the straight culture inhibited sexuality and postponed gratification then the counter-culture wanted to flaunt sex and have it all now and often. Theirs was a children's crusade of pop hedonism that created almost nothing and left only litter in its wake.[30]

All such denunciations are true up to a point. The counter-culture and the student rebels were as one-dimensional as the culture they opposed, but at least theirs was the antithesis, the missing ingredient in *The Organization Man* or the Whizz-Kids who succeeded in killing some 2.5 million Vietnamese in the deluded belief that Communism spells doom. The media tends to turn such clashes into sound-bites and stereotyped confrontations with flowers placed in the barrels of guns. The polarity is instantly recognizable while the mingling and subtle syntheses of these streams are not. The 'Bourgeois' and the 'Bohemian' are unrecognizable to either of these former adversaries once they merge. Florida comments:

> The cultural legacy of the Sixties as it turned out was not Woodstock after all, but something new ... Silicon Valley, the place in the very heart of the San Francisco Bay Area, became the proving ground for a new ethic of creativity. Work needed to be 'aesthetic' and experiential ... spiritual and 'useful' in the poetic senses rather than the duty-bound sense.[31]

What Silicon Valley provided was what the movement had lacked to that point, an economic base, plus electronic tools that were to transform business-as-usual and restore power to the person. The personal computer was seen as a tool of liberation. Apple depicted IBM employees in lock-step shuffling to their doom, with the corporate computer personified as Big Brother, appearing briefly on a screen before it was shattered by a female hammer-thrower. The story is well told in *Fire in the Valley: The Making of the Personal Computer* by Paul Freiberger and Michael Swaine.[32] Frederick Moore recently transferred from the *Berkeley Barb* and the Peace Movement helped to lead the Homebrew Club, where the early computer buffs plotted their revolution. Apple T-shirts of the time read 'Working 90 hours a week and loving it'. A new movement was in the making.

One reason that engineering suddenly became 'hip', although engineering students had been scarce in the Free Speech Movement, was the joining of popular music with new ways of amplifying and blending it. The music synthesizer synthesized more than music. It wove hard into soft, science into art and codified impulse. The 'geek' came out of the cold to become a cultural icon. The younger generation had found powerful tools at which they were more adept, as hackers exposed secret databases.

With the benefit of hindsight we can recognize that most of the sixties' revolts were *ad hoc*, more cultural than political, with socialism and Marxism espoused by only a small minority. The French students' revolt in Paris in May 1968 was half-playful with postures of entertaining artistry. Mottoes like 'I am a Marxist of the Groucho variety' or 'Beneath the pavements the beach' told of a society where self-fulfilment and fun had been drilled out of young people and they intended to enjoy themselves. When Florida interviewed members of the creative class they rejected labels like Bourgeois and Bohemian, straight culture or counter-culture, conservative or radical. It was not that they denied these influences in their pasts but that they felt trivialized by such labels. They had moved beyond this to their own potent synthesis and it was this they wanted to describe.

(H) IS THIS CLASS NOW IN FLIGHT FROM AMERICA?
Florida followed up *The Rise of the Creative Class* with *The Flight of the Creative Class*.[33] The influence of this class had begun ebbing under the premiership of George W. Bush and his visceral dislike of all things creative and unfamiliar. Tom Daley, a Republican leader in Congress, described Nobel Prize winners as 'a bunch of liberals'. Certainly those parts of the nation containing the bulk of the creative class voted against Bush by land-slide proportions. His cabinet lacked any representative of 'new' businesses in electronics, biology or computers. A 'class war' against irreligious and creative life-styles was the theme of two election campaigns.

Florida reports a set of grim trends which suggest the USA is losing its former pre-eminence, while other nations step into the gap. London, Paris, Frankfurt, Sydney, Toronto, Zurich and Seoul are centres where the creative class gather. Amsterdam, Caracas, Stockholm, Geneva, Jakarta, Osaka, Taipei, Montreal, Bangkok, Beijing, Helsinki, Kuala Lumpur, Bangalore and Shanghai are rapidly increasing their appeal to this class. Countries like Singapore have deliberately created street-level culture around 'Biopolis' and 'Fusionopolis' and allowed gays into civil service jobs. Dublin has helped Ireland become the second largest software exporter in the world.[34]

America's major weakness is its rabid polarization of almost every argument into good vs. evil, what Deborah Tannen calls *The Argument Culture*,[35] with its win/lose stereotypical extremes. The problem with ideological polarization is its sterility. Creativity lies somewhere between, but both conflicting parties eschew any concessions. Yes, much of the counter-culture was a flaunting of make-believe, but we need dreams to be innovative. We need to imagine how things might be. Florida fears that America is closing itself off. America fails to see economic development as a 'learning race', otherwise it would not so readily outsource its cheaper manufacturing to a global supply chain, which also involves outsourcing key rungs on the knowledge ladder, which its own citizens cannot then climb. Foreign business is only too willing to climb these rungs and as we saw earlier is 'hollowing out' the core competence of many multinationals, offering to do more and more as they learn.

America's traditional strength has been the diversity of foreign students it allowed into the country. By 2001 one-quarter of science and engineering graduates in the USA were foreign born. Nearly half of those granted PhDs in computer sciences, life sciences and physical sciences were foreigners. One-third of the Nobel Prizes won by US universities from 1985 to 1999 were awarded to foreign scientists.

Yet all this leaves America very vulnerable. One reason for this reliance on foreigners is that American primary and secondary education lags behind that of other nations. America educates Masters and Doctoral students from abroad because its own students are not coming forward in sufficient numbers and because the qualifications of foreigners are better. If for any reason foreigners stopped coming, the resulting skills famine could be catastrophic to the US economy and decimate the creative class. But following on 9/11 and America's pre-emptive wars in Iraq and Afghanistan, this is what has happened. America is faced with a reverse brain-drain. Not only are foreigners not coming, but those already in the US are being attracted home again by their burgeoning economies in China, India and the Pacific Rim. Many now decide not to come at all, so fast are their own economies expanding.

Florida's thesis makes grim reading. From 2002 to 2003 the number of visiting scholars to the USA declined for the first time in a decade, as did the number of foreign researchers working for the National Institutes for Health. The number of visas granted to foreign scientists dropped a whopping 55% according to the National Science Board and has not recovered. Visa applications to America by foreign students dropped by nearly 20% between 2001 and 2003, or by 74,000, while visas for those of unusually high skills dropped by more than 20%. The total number of visas to the USA had declined by 40% by 2003, from 6.3 million to 3.7 million, while applications fell by 100,000. Although fewer apply, a greater proportion is rejected. The rejection rate rose from 9.5% to 17.8% in the 'high skill' category alone.[36]

A 2004 study of American institutions of higher education shows a 47% decline in foreign graduate student applications and a 36% decline in undergraduate applications. All this is exacerbated by the shifting choices in what Americans choose to study at college and graduate school. The 'hard slog' subjects like physics, chemistry, biology, mathematics and even computer sciences are being sidestepped in favour of less hard and demanding disciplines. In the hard sciences there is more and more to learn and the long march to the frontiers of knowledge grows ever longer. East Asians tend to specialize here, because right or wrong answers protect them from prejudice by Western teachers and because the nations they come from stress these basic disciplines. Yet American students may be avoiding these burdensome subjects.[37]

SUMMARY: THE CREATIVE CLASS AND THE RESOLUTION OF CONTRASTING VALUES

We have seen in this exploration of the rise of a creative class that contrasting values, or dilemmas, have been reconciled to generate something new. This has been the underlying logic of this entire book. We saw that the changes occurring in the second half of the twentieth century and up to this time have largely been changes in norms and values through the never-ending process of combining these.

We saw that creativity comes from clusters of persons of great individuality, that creativity is driven by ideas but in new combinations of these, that such persons are managed largely by themselves. Theirs is a disciplined freedom, however, with science and aesthetics as their authority. This is a serious form of combinatory play. *Homo creativus* is a rebel who submits to Nature. While the economic law of decreasing returns is all around us, ideas and innovation provide increasing returns.

The creative class makes the greatest contribution to the economy, over and above its numbers. It moves beyond scarcity into abundance, yet its products once created are scarce and hence valuable. While in many ways privileged, it sympathizes with the outsider and the deprived. It is characterized by an egalitarian elitism, treating as equals diverse persons of distinction. They consume experiences so they can produce novel experiences themselves as 'prosumers'. They are often said to be a fusion of Bourgeois and Bohemian although they dislike both terms.

At work they are most attracted not by money but by challenge, which elicits from them skilled activities that are self-fulfilling. They like to join the 'machine shop' with the 'hair salon', engineering work with conviviality. While they persevere in solving problems they like to be flexible also. Ironically, it is mobility between jobs that allows them to remain committed to lines of discovery. In their offices they like a place of their own with plenty of meeting spaces.

Their employers expect them to fail but to get it right in the end by the process of correcting errors. The office mimics the home so they feel at home at work and at work at home, maintaining the warm intimacy of the primary group and continuing to create in both settings. Managers wander about but harvest ideas in this process. While employees have a role they are expected to change this into something new to meet challenges. While they work for pay, in another sense they are volunteers in finding problems and solving these for the pleasure inherent in the process of doing so. They are subject to the soft controls of peer pressure and their own promises. They are not burned out because the workplace also refreshes them.

196 IS A NEW CREATIVE CLASS ARISING?

They work long hours yet the sense of time collapses for them as they enjoy a flow experience of categories fusing. Work ceases to be exploitative when it is enjoyed. To save time they work in parallel processes then fuse these lines of endeavour. They also combine mind and body through physical fitness and sport for the sheer experience of this. They prefer to set their own rules. For them games are infinite not adversarial.

The origins of the creative class may lie in the Berkeley Free Speech Movement of 1964 and the succession of student revolts which married rebellion to scholarship, defiance of Nature to respect for it. The counter-culture took the values of the dominant culture and contradicted them all. Was this a revolt of consumers, soft and pampered, against producers? Perhaps, but the synthesis created artistic engineers around the music industry and advocates of the personal computer against the corporate computer. It was largely a life-style rebellion against educational institutions still teaching compliance, the results of which could be seen in Vietnam.

There is a danger of America losing its competitive advantage, because to reduce diversity is to sacrifice the new combinations that can be made from these diverse elements. This sterility finds its symptoms in America's conservative backlash and in the highly polarized 'argument culture'. Yet America's problems mean gains for the rest of the world. The creative class is spreading across the globe.

Notes

Introduction

1 Kaplan, Abraham (1964), *The Conduct of Inquiry*, San Francisco: Chandler.
2 Koestler, Arthur (1964), *The Act of Creation*, New York: Macmillan, has an excellent discussion on creativity in general.
3 Gordon, William J. J. (1961), *Synectics: The Development of Creative Capacity*, New York: Harper and Row.
4 Watson, James D. (2001), *The Double Helix: A Personal Account of the Discovery of DNA*, New York: Touchstone.
5 Hagen, Everett (1962), *On the Theory of Social Change: How Economic Growth Begins*, Homewood, IL: Dorsey Press.
6 Hurst, David K. (1995), *Crisis and Renewal*, Boston, MA: Harvard Business School Publishing.
7 Saxenian, Anna Lee (1999), *Silicon Valley's New Immigrant Entrepreneurs*, San Francisco: Public Policy Institute of California.
8 See especially attempts by the British Government's School Inspectorate to close down Summerhill which failed in the court.

Chapter 1

1 Kian, Teo Ming (2008), 'Empowering Technopreneurs', *The World in 2008: Economist Year Book*, pp. 113–22.
2 Kao, John (2007), *Innovation Nation*, New York: Free Press, pp. 55–8.
3 Koh, Buck Song, (ed.) (2004), *Heartwork*, Singapore: EDB, and personal communication with Teo Ming Kian.
4 GEM Studies are available from Babson College, Massachusetts and from the London Business School.
5 Koh (2004).
6 Hampden-Turner, C. M., and Tan Teng-Kee (2002), 'Six Dilemmas of Entrepreneurship', *Singapore Nanyang Business Review* 1:2 (December 2002), pp. 78–96.
7 Saxenian, Anna Lee (1999), *Silicon Valley's New Immigrant Entrepreneurs*, San Francisco: Public Policy Institute of California.

8 Early and late developers are discussed in most psychological texts e.g. Gross, Richard D. (1992), *Psychology: The Science of Mind and Behaviour*, London: Hodder and Stoughton, Chapters 19 and 23.

9 Kian (2008).

10 Schön, Donald A. (1985), *The Reflective Practitioner*, New York: Harper Torchbooks.

Chapter 2

1 Guilford, J. P. (1959), *Creativity and its Cultivation*, New York, Harper and Row. See also Paul E. Plsek (1997), *Creativity, Innovation, and Quality*, Milwaukee, WI: ASQC Quality Press.

2 Bateson, Gregory (2000), *Steps to an Ecology of Mind*, Chicago: University of Chicago Press, pp. 14–20.

3 Huizinga, John (1970), *Homo Ludens: A Study of the Play Element in Culture*, New York: Harper. This is the classic exposition of the civilizing role of playing. It permits cultures to simulate non-injuriously tragedy, comedy or drama in general: if you cannot laugh at yourself you will shortly weep!

4 Quoted by Kelley, Tom (2002), in *The Art of Innovation*, New York: Random House.

5 See Gordon (1961).

6 Personal communication.

7 Kao (2007).

8 Saxenian (1999).

9 Florida, Richard (2002), *The Rise of the Creative Class*, New York: Basic Books.

10 Slywotzky, Adrian, and Richard Wise (2003), *How to Grow When Markets Don't*, New York: Warner Business Books.

11 Toffler, Alvin (1980), *The Third Wave*, New York: Bantam Books.

12 Trompenaars, Fons, and Charles Hampden-Turner (2001), *21 Leaders for the 21st Century*, Oxford: Capstone, pp. 125–40.

13 Christiansen, Clayton (1999), *The Innovator's Dilemma*, Boston, MA: Harvard Business School Press.

Chapter 3

1 Koestler, Arthur (1964), *The Act of Creation*, New York: Macmillan.

2 Gordon (1961).

3 Maslow, Abraham (1954), *Motivation and Personality*, New York: Harper.

4 *Ibid.*, p. 121.

5 Campbell, Joseph, (ed.) (1971), *The Portable Jung*, New York: Viking.

6 Rogers, Carl (1961), *On Becoming a Person*, Boston: Houghton Mifflin.

7 Buber, Martin (1970), *I and Thou*, New York: Charles Scribner.

8 Csikszentmihalyi, Mihaly (1990), *Flow: The Psychology of Optimal Experience*, New York: Harper.

9 Maslow, Abraham (1962), *Towards a Psychology of Being*, New York: Van Nostrand.

10 de Bono, Edward (1994), *Water Logic*, London: Penguin.

11 Pribram, Karl (1971), *Languages of the Brain*, Englewood Cliffs, NJ: Prentice Hall.

12 Maslow (1962).

13 Blake, William (1794), 'The Poison Tree', from *Songs of Experience*.

14 Capra, Fritjof (2002), *The Hidden Connections*, New York: Doubleday. The author is a physicist by training and is enlightening on the social scientific implications of the new physics.

15 Bogen, J. E. (1975), one of the pioneer surgeons in splitting the brain, is particularly interesting on the educational implications; see 'Some Educational Aspects of Hemispheric Specialization', *UCLA Educator* 17 (Spring 1975), pp. 24–32.

Chapter 4

1 Goleman, Daniel (1995), *Emotional Intelligence*, London: Bloomsbury.

2 Diven, K. (1937), 'Certain Determinants in the Conditioning of Anxiety Reactions', *Journal of Abnormal and Social Psychology* 3 (1937), pp. 291–305, quoted and discussed by White, Robert (1982), *The Abnormal Personality*, New York: Basic Books, p. 200.

3 Ebrey, Patricia Buckley (1996), *The Cambridge Illustrated History of China*, Cambridge: Cambridge University Press.

4 Barron, Frank (1968), *Creativity and Personal Freedom*, New York: Van Nostrand, pp. 31–2.

5 Adshead, S. A. M. (2004), *T'ang China*, New York: Palgrave Macmillan. See also Kynge, James (2006), *China Shakes the World*, London: Weidenfeld and Nicolson, pp. 37–9.

6 Johansson, Frans (2004), *The Medici Effect*, Boston, MA: Harvard Business School Publishing.

7 Hurst (1995), Chapter 1.

8 Schrage, Michael (2000), *Serious Play*, Boston, MA: Harvard Business School Publishing.

9 Huizinga (1970), p. 231.
10 Csikszentmihalyi (1990), p. 33.
11 Toffler (1980), p. 66.
12 Kaplan (1964), Chapter 1.
13 Quoted by Matson, Floyd (1964), *The Broken Image*, New York: Braziller, p. 46.

Chapter 5
1 Ebrey (1996), p. 233.
2 Barron, Frank, Alfonso Montuori, and Anthea Barron (eds.) (1997), *Creators on Creating*, New York: Jeremy Tarcher/Putnam.
3 Kelley (2002).
4 Schrage (2000).
5 Quoted *ibid.*, p. 11.
6 Kuhn, Thomas (1970), *The Structure of Scientific Revolutions*, Chicago: University of Chicago Press.
7 de Bono, Edward (1982), *Lateral Thinking*, Harmondsworth: Penguin.
8 Russell, Bertrand (1947), *New Ideas in a Changing World*, London: Heinemann.

Chapter 6
1 Kynge, James (2006), *China Shakes the World*, London: Weidenfeld and Nicolson, pp. 209–11.
2 Kuhn (1970).
3 Yinke, Deng (2005), *Ancient Chinese Inventions*, Beijing: China Intercontinental Press.

Chapter 7
1 Bateson (2000), pp. 61–88.
2 Kolb, David (1985), *Learning Style Inventory*, Boston, MA: McBer and Co.
3 Personal communication.
4 Groen, Bram, and Charles Hampden-Turner (2005), *The Titans of Saturn*, London: Cyan Communications.
5 Schrage (2000), Chapter 4.
6 *Ibid.*
7 Toffler (1980), Chapter 3.
8 Enriquez, Juan (2001), *As the Future Catches You*, New York: Three Rivers Press, pp. 88–102.

9 Tannen, Deborah (1990), *You Just Don't Understand*, New York: Ballantine.
10 de Bono (1982).

Chapter 8

1 Trompenaars, Fons, and Charles Hampden-Turner (2004), *Managing People Across Cultures*, Chichester: Capstone, pp. 6–15.
2 Roethlisberger, Fritz, and William Dixon (1939), *Management and the Worker*, Cambridge, MA: Harvard University Press.
3 See Hampden-Turner, Charles (1973), *Radical Man: Towards a Theory of Psycho-Social Development*, London: Duckworth, especially Chapter 1, 'The Borrowed Toolbox and Conservative Man'.
4 A good description of this experiment can be found in Kretch, David, R. S. Crutchfield, and E. L. Ballachey (1962), *Individual in Society*, New York: McGraw-Hill.
5 Milgram, Stanley (1963), 'Behavioural Study of Obedience', *Journal of Abnormal and Social Psychology* 67:4, pp. 371–8.
6 Zimbardo, Philip (2007), *The Lucifer Effect: How Good People Turn Evil*, London: Rider.
7 Rapaport, Anatol (1964), *Strategy and Conscience*, New York: Harper. The author argues that strategy and human conscience belong to different worlds.
8 Orwell, George (1949), *Nineteen Eighty-Four*, London: Secker & Warburg, Part 3, Chapters 5 and 6.

Chapter 9

1 Kelley (2002).
2 Kao (2007).
3 Christiansen (1999).
4 Wright, Robert (2000), *NonZero: The Logic of Human Destiny*, New York: Pantheon Books.

Chapter 10

1 Toffler (1980), Chapter 1.
2 More specifically the Harvard Program on Technology and Society, the Wright Institute (at one time a centre in Stanford), Strawberry Creek College, an inter-disciplinary programme at UC Berkeley, and Nanyang Technopreneurship Center at NTU.

3 McClelland, David (1961), *The Achieving Society*, Princeton, NJ: Van Nostrand, p. 603.
4 Christiansen (1999), p. 26.
5 Florida (2002), pp. 48–55.
6 Trompenaars, Fons, and Charles Hampden-Turner (2001), *21 Leaders for the 21st Century*, Oxford: Capstone, pp. 125–40.
7 Dearlove, Desmond (1998), *The Richard Branson Way*, Oxford: Capstone.
8 Peters, Tom, and R. H. Waterman (1982), *In Search of Excellence*, New York: Harper and Row.
9 Personal communication at Harvard Business School.
10 Personal communication at Judge Business School.
11 McClelland (1961), p. 212.

Chapter 11

1 Hawken, Paul, Amory Lovins and L. Hunter Lovins (1999), *Natural Capitalism*, Boston: Little Brown. See in particular Chapter 2, 'Re-inventing the Wheels'. See also Hawken, Paul (1993), *The Ecology of Commerce*, New York: Harper Business, pp. 37–57.
2 Huntington, Samuel P. (1996), *The Clash of Civilizations and the Remaking of World Order*, New York: Simon & Schuster.
3 Trompenaars, Fons (2008), *Riding the Whirlwind*, Oxford: Infinite Ideas Co., pp. 10–21.
4 Slywotzky and Wise (2003).
5 Florida (2002), pp. 255–8.
6 Maslow, Abraham (1998), *Maslow on Management*, New York: John Wiley, p. 231.
7 Carse, James P. (1986), *Finite and Infinite Games*, New York: Ballantine; see also Hampden-Turner, Charles, and Fons Trompenaars (1997), *Mastering the Infinite Game*, Oxford: Capstone.
8 Johansson (2004).
9 Bacon, Francis, *The Great Instauration*, quoted by Jonas, Hans (1959), in 'The Practical Uses of Theory', *Social Research* 26:2.
10 Nye, Joseph S. (2004), *Soft Power: The Means to Success in World Politics*, New York: Public Affairs.
11 Florida, Richard (2005), *The Flight of the Creative Class*, New York: Harper Business.
12 Dawkins, Richard (2008), *The God Delusion*, London: Black Swan.
13 Bateson (2000), pp. 346–63.

14 Chen, Ming-Jer (2001), *Inside Chinese Business*, Boston: Harvard Business School Press, pp. 92–8.
15 Quoted by Chen (2001), p. 201.
16 Prahalad, C. K., and Venkat Ramswamy (2004), *The Future of Competition: Co-creating Unique Value with Customers*, Boston: Harvard Business School Press, is a good example.
17 Kim, Chan W., and Renée Mauborgne (2005), *Blue Ocean Strategy*, Boston, MA: Harvard Business School Press.
18 Tatsuno, Sheridan (1990), *Created in Japan*, New York: Harper and Row.

Chapter 12
1 Florida (2002).
2 *Ibid.*, pp. 4–5.
3 Reich, Robert B. (1991), *The Work of Nations*, New York: Alfred Knopf.
4 Florida (2002), p. 6.
5 *Ibid.*, pp. 8–12.
6 See Cortright, Joseph (2000), *New Growth Theory*, Washington, DC: US Economic Development Administation.
7 Quoted in Florida (2002), p. 32.
8 Jacobs, Jane (1961), *Death and Life of Great American Cities*, New York: Random House.
9 Florida (2002), p. 33.
10 *Ibid.*, p. 46.
11 *Ibid.*, p. 51.
12 *Ibid.*, pp. 255–8.
13 Brooks, David (2001), *Bobos in Paradise*, New York: Simon & Schuster.
14 Florida (2002), p. 89.
15 *Ibid.*, pp. 125–6.
16 Peters and Waterman (1982).
17 Drucker, Peter (1993), *Post-Capitalist Society*, New York: Harper Business, pp. 7–11.
18 Whyte, William (1956), *The Organization Man*, New York: Simon & Schuster.
19 Weber, Steve (2004), *The Success of Open Source*, Cambridge, MA: Harvard University Press.
20 Amabile, Theresa (1996), *Creativity in Context*, Boulder, CO: Westview Press.
21 Personal communication.

22 Kelley (2002).

23 Csikszentmihalyi (1990), p. 123.

24 Florida (2002), pp. 110–32.

25 Toffler (1980), p. 26.

26 Florida (2002), pp. 170–8.

27 *Men's Fitness* (Jan. 2001) quoted in Florida (2002), p. 177.

28 Jung, Carl Gustav (1971), *Collected Works*, Princeton: Princeton University Press.

29 Bell, Daniel (1976), *The Cultural Contradictions of Capitalism*, New York: Basic Books.

30 *Ibid.*, pp. 86–95.

31 Florida (2002), pp. 201–9.

32 Freiberger, Paul, and Michael Swaine (1986), *Fire in the Valley: The Making of the Personal Computer*, Berkeley, CA: Osborne/McGraw-Hill, pp. 17–19.

33 Florida, Richard (2005), *The Flight of the Creative Class*, New York: Harper Business.

34 Kao (2007), pp. 55–8.

35 Tannen, Deborah (1998), *The Argument Culture*, New York: Random House.

36 Florida (2005), pp. 110–32.

37 Christiansen, Clayton, personal communication.

Bibliography

Adshead, S. A. M. (2004), *T'ang China*, New York: Palgrave Macmillan.

Amabile, Theresa (1996), *Creativity in Context*, Boulder, CO: Westview Press.

Argyris, C. (1980), *The Concept of Rigorous Research*, New York: Academic Press.

(1986), 'Skilled Incompetence', *Harvard Business Review*, September/October.

Barron, Frank (1968), *Creativity and Personal Freedom*, New York: Van Nostrand.

Barron, Frank, Alfonso Montiori, and Anthea Barron (1997), *Creators on Creating*, New York: Jeremy Tarcher/Putnam.

Bartlett, Christopher A., and Sumantra Ghoshal (1991), *Managing Across Borders*, Boston, MA: Harvard Business School Press.

Bateson, Gregory (2000), *Steps to an Ecology of Mind*, Chicago: University of Chicago Press.

Bateson, M. C. (1991), *Our Own Metaphor*, Washington, DC: Smithsonian Institution Press.

Becker, Ernest (1973), *The Denial of Death*, New York: Free Press.

Bell, D. (1976), *The Cultural Contradictions of Capitalism*, New York: Basic Books.

Benedict, R. (1934), *Patterns of Culture*, Boston: Houghton Mifflin.

Blake, William (1794), 'The Poison Tree', in *Songs of Experience*.

Bogen, J. E. (1975), 'Some Educational Aspects of Hemispheric Specialization', *UCLA Educator* 17 (Spring 1975), pp. 24–32.

de Bono, Edward (1982), *Lateral Thinking*, London: Penguin.

(1994), *Water Logic*, London: Penguin.

Brandenburger, A., and B. J. Nalebuff (1996), *Coopetition*, New York: Doubleday.

Brooks, David (2001), *Bobos in Pardise*, New York: Simon & Schuster.

Buber, Martin (1970), *I and Thou*, New York: Charles Scribner.

Campbell, Joseph, (ed.) (1971), *The Portable Jung*, New York: Viking.

Capra, Fritjof (2002), *The Hidden Connections*, New York: Doubleday.

Carse, James P. (1986), *Finite and Infinite Games*, New York: Ballantine.

Chen, Ming-Jer (2001), *Inside Chinese Business*, Boston, MA: Harvard Business School Press.

Christiansen, Clayton (1999), *The Innovator's Dilemma*, Boston, MA: Harvard Business School Press.

Cortright, Joseph (2000), *New Growth Theory*, Washington, DC: US Economic Development Administration.

Csikszentmihalyi, Mihaly (1990), *Flow: The Psychology of Optimal Experience*, New York: Harper.

Dawkins, Richard (2008), *The God Delusion*, London: Black Swan.

Dearlove, Desmond (1998), *The Richard Branson Way*, Oxford: Capstone.

Diven, K. (1937), 'Certain Determinants in the Conditioning of Anxiety Reactions', *Journal of Abnormal and Social Psychology* 3, pp. 291–305.

Drucker, Peter (1993), *Post-Capitalist Society*, New York: Harper Business.

(1999), 'Knowledge Worker Productivity: The Biggest Challenge', *California Management Review* 41:2, pp. 79–94.

Ebrey, Patricia Buckley (1996), *The Cambridge Illustrated History of China*, Cambridge: Cambridge University Press.

Enriquez, Juan (2001), *As the Future Catches You*, New York: Three Rivers Press.

Evans, Paul, Y. Doz and A. Laurent (eds.) (1989), *Human Resource Management in International Firms*, New York: Macmillan Press.

Florida, Richard (2002), *The Rise of the Creative Class and How It's Transforming Work, Life, Community, and Everyday Life*, New York: Basic Books.

(2005), *The Flight of the Creative Class*, New York: Harper Business.

Freiberger, Paul, and Michael Swaine (1986), *Fire in the Valley: The Making of the Personal Computer*, Berkeley, CA: Osborne/McGraw-Hill.

Getzels, J. W., and P. W. Jackson (1962), *Creativity and Intelligence: Explorations with Gifted Students*, New York: Wiley.

Goleman, Daniel (1995), *Emotional Intelligence*, London: Bloomsbury.

Gordon, William J. J. (1961), *Synectics: The Development of Creative Capacity*, New York: Harper and Row.

Groen, Bram, and Charles Hampden-Turner (2005), *The Titans of Saturn*, London: Cyan Communications.

Gross, Richard D. (1992), *Psychology: The Science of Mind and Behaviour*, London: Hodder & Stoughton.

Guilford, J. P. (1959), *Creativity and its Cultivation*, New York: Harper and Row.

Hagen, Everett (1962), *On the Theory of Social Change: How Economic Growth Begins*, Homewood, IL: Dorsey Press.

Hampden-Turner, Charles M. (1973), *Radical Man: Towards a Theory of Psycho-Social Development*, London: Duckworth.

(1974), *Sane Asylum: Inside the Delancey Street Foundation*, New York: William Morrow.

(1981), *Maps of the Mind*, New York: Macmillan.

(1984), *Gentlemen and Tradesmen*, London: Routledge and Kegan Paul.

(1985), 'Approaching Dilemmas', *Shell Guides to Planning*, no. 3.

(1992), *Creating Corporate Culture*, Reading, MA: Addison-Wesley.

(1994), *Charting the Corporate Mind: From Dilemma to Strategy*, Oxford: Basil Blackwell.

Hampden-Turner, C. M., and Fons Trompenaars (1997), *Mastering the Infinite Game*, Oxford: Capstone.

Hampden-Turner, C. M., and Tan Teng-Kee (2002), 'Six Dilemmas of Entrepreneurship: Can Singapore Transform Itself to Become an Innovative Economy?', *Nanyang Business Review* 1:2 (July–December), pp. 78–96.

Handy, C. (1984), *The Age of Paradox*, Boston, MA: Harvard Business School Press.

Hawken, Paul (1993), *The Ecology of Commerce*, New York: Harper Business.

Hawken, Paul, Amory Lovins and L. Hunter Lovins (1999), *Natural Capitalism*, Boston, MA: Little Brown.

Huizinga, J. (1970), *Homo Ludens: A Study of the Play Element in Culture*, New York: Harper.

Hurst, D. K. (1984), 'Of Boxes, Bubbles and Effective Management', *Harvard Business Review*, May/June.

(1995), *Crisis and Renewal*, Boston, MA: Harvard Business School Press.

Huntington, Samuel P. (1996), *The Clash of Civilizations and the Remaking of World Order*, New York: Simon & Schuster.

Jacobi, J. (1973), *The Psychology of C. G. Jung*, New Haven: Yale University Press.

Jacobs, Jane (1961), *The Death and Life of Great American Cities*, New York: Random House.

Johansson, Frans (2004), *The Medici Effect*, Boston, MA: Harvard Business School Publishing.

Jonas, Hans (1959), 'The Practical Uses of Theory', *Social Research* 26:2.

Jung, Carl Gustav (1971), *Collected Works*, Princeton, NJ: Princeton University Press.

Kao, John (1996), *Jamming: The Art and Discipline of Business Creativity*, New York: Harper Business.

(2007), *Innovation Nation*, New York: Free Press.

Kaplan, Abraham (1964), *The Conduct of Inquiry*, San Francisco, CA: Chandler.

Kelley, Tom (2002), *The Art of Innovation*, New York: Random House.

Kim, Chan W., and Renée Mauborgne (2005), *Blue Ocean Strategy*, Boston, MA: Harvard Business School Press.

King, Martin Luther (1963), *Why We Can't Wait*, New York: Harper and Row.

Koestler, Arthur (1964), *The Act of Creation*, New York: Macmillan.

Koh, Buck Song, (ed.) (2004), *Heartwork*, Singapore: EDB.

Kolb, D. (1985), *Learning Style Inventory*, Boston, MA: McBer Co.

Kretch, David, Robert Crutchfield, and E. L. Ballachey (1962), *Individual in Society*, New York: McGraw-Hill.

Kuhn, Thomas (1970), *The Structure of Scientific Revolutions*, Chicago: University of Chicago Press.

Kynge, James (2006), *China Shakes the World*, London: Weidenfeld and Nicolson.

Lévi-Strauss, Claude (1955), 'The Structural Study of Myth', *Journal of American Folklore* 68:20, pp. 428–44.

(1979), *Structural Anthropology*, New York: Penguin.

Lewin, Kurt (1951), *Field Theory in Social Science*, New York: Harper.

Marrow, Alfred (1969), *The Practical Theorist: The Psychology of Kurt Lewin*, New York: Basic Books.

Maslow, Abraham (1954), *Motivation and Personality*, New York: Harper.

(1962), *Towards a Psychology of Being*, New York: Van Nostrand.

(1998), *Maslow on Management*, New York: John Wiley.

Matson, Floyd (1964), *The Broken Image*, New York: Braziller.

McClelland, David (1961), *The Achieving Society*, Princeton, NJ: Van Nostrand.

Milgram, Stanley (1963), 'Behavioural Study of Obedience', *Journal of Abnormal and Social Psychology* 67:4, pp. 371–8.

Mintzberg, H. (1989), 'Crafting Strategy', *Harvard Business Review*, March/April, pp. 66–75.

Nonaka, I., and H. Takeuchi (1995), *The Knowledge-Creating Company*, New York: Oxford University Press.

Nye, Joseph S. (2004), *Soft Power: The Means to Success in World Politics*, New York: Public Affairs.

Peters, Tom, and R. H. Waterman (1982), *In Search of Excellence*, New York: Harper and Row.

Pine, Joseph P. (1993), *Mass Customization*, Boston, MA: Harvard Business School Press.

Plsek, Paul E. (1997), *Creativity, Innovation and Quality*, Milwaukee, WI: ASQC Press.

Prahalad, C. K., and Venkat Ramaswamy (2004), *The Future of Competition: Co-creating Unique Value with Customers*, Boston, MA: Harvard Business School Press.

Pribram, Karl (1971), *Languages of the Brain*, Englewood Cliffs, NJ: Prentice Hall.

Rapaport, Anatol (1964), *Strategy and Conscience*, New York: Harper.

Reich, Robert B. (1991), *The Work of Nations*, New York: Alfred Knopf.

Roethlisberger, Fritz, and William Dixon (1939), *Management and the Worker*, Cambridge, MA: Harvard University Press.

Rogers, Carl (1961), *On Becoming a Person*, Boston: Houghton Mifflin.

Russell, Bertrand (1947), *New Ideas in a Changing World*, London: Heinemann.

Saxenian, Anna Lee (1999), *Silicon Valley's New Immigrant Entrepreneurs*, San Francisco: Public Policy Institute of California.

Schön, Donald A. (1985), *The Reflective Practitioner*, New York: Harper Torchbooks.

Schrage, Michael (2000), *Serious Play*, Boston, MA: Harvard Business School Press.

Schumpeter, Joseph A. ([1942] 1975), 'Creative Destruction', in *Capitalism, Socialism and Democracy*, New York: Harper, pp. 82–5.

Sculley, John, and J. A. Byrne (1987), *Odyssey: Pepsi to Apple: A Journey of Adventure, Ideas and the Future*, New York: HarperCollins.

Slywotzky, Adrian, and Richard Wise (2003), *How to Grow When Markets Don't*, New York: Warner Business Books.

Sperry, Roger W. (1964), 'The Great Cerebral Commissure', *Scientific American* 410 (January), pp. 42–52.

Tannen, Deborah (1990), *You Just Don't Understand*, New York: Ballantine Books.

(1998), *The Argument Culture*, New York: Random House.

Tatsuno, Sheridan M. (1990), *Created in Japan*, New York: Morrow.

Toffler, Alvin (1970), *Future Shock*, New York: Bantam Books.

(1980), *The Third Wave*, New York: Bantam Books.

Toynbee, Arnold J. (1934–54), *A Study of History*, 10 vols., Oxford: Oxford University Press.

Trompenaars, Fons (2008), *Riding the Whirlwind*, Oxford: Infinite Ideas Co.

Trompenaars, Fons, and Charles Hampden-Turner (1998), *Riding the Waves of Culture*, New York: McGraw-Hill.

(2001), *21 Leaders for the 21st Century*, Oxford: Capstone.

(2002), *Managing People Across Cultures*, Oxford: Capstone.

Wang, Wei (2006), *The China Executive: Marrying Chinese and Western Strengths*, Peterborough: 2W Publishing.

Watson, James D. (2001), *The Double Helix: A Personal Account of the Discovery of DNA*, New York: Touchstone.

Weber, Steve (2004), *The Success of Open Source*, Cambridge, MA: Harvard University Press.

White, Robert W. (1982), *The Abnormal Personality*, New York: Basic Books.

Whyte, William (1956), *The Organization Man*, New York: Simon & Schuster.

Wright, Robert (2000), *NonZero: The Logic of Human Destiny*, New York: Pantheon Books.

Yinke, Deng (2005), *Ancient Chinese Inventions*, Beijing: China Intercontinental Press.

Zimbardo, Philip (2007), *The Lucifer Effect: How Good People Turn Evil*, London: Rider.

Appendix I

The number of respondents who scored NTU and TIP in the polarized zones of the Grid (Top Left) (X≤3∩Y≥8) 11(Questions)×68(persons)=748

Top-Left	NTU	%	TIP	%
Q1	11	16.18%	0	0.00%
Q2	20	29.41%	0	0.00%
Q3	15	22.06%	0	0.00%
Q4	15	22.06%	1	1.47%
Q5	17	25.00%	1	1.47%
Q6	14	20.59%	0	0.00%
Q7	10	14.71%	2	2.94%
Q8	12	17.65%	0	0.00%
Q9	16	23.53%	0	0.00%
Q10	19	27.94%	0	0.00%
Q11	22	32.35%	1	1.47%
Total	**171**	**22.86%**	**5**	**0.67%**

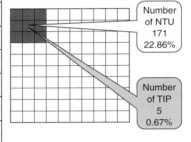

Number of NTU
171
22.86%

Number of TIP
5
0.67%

The number of respondents who scored NTU and TIP in the polarized zones of the Grid (Bottom right) (X ≤ 8∩Y ≥ 3) 11(Questions)×68 (persons)= 748

Bottom-Right	NTU	%	TIP	%
Q1	0	0.00%	3	4.41%
Q2	0	0.00%	4	5.88%
Q3	1	1.47%	2	2.94%
Q4	0	0.00%	3	4.41%
Q5	1	1.47%	7	10.29%
Q6	0	0.00%	3	4.41%
Q7	2	2.94%	3	4.41%
Q8	1	1.47%	2	2.94%
Q9	0	0.00%	3	4.41%
Q10	1	1.47%	4	5.88%
Q11	1	1.47%	9	13.24%
Total	**7**	**0.94%**	**43**	**5.75%**

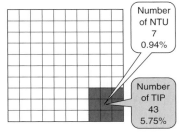

We believe it possible for education to become perilously unbalanced. For example, students may be able to memorize intellectual codes presented to them but be incapable of understanding their own experience. They could be swamped in experience but be unable to order this intellectually. We therefore tested university courses for Top-Heaviness (see red square at top left) and we tested TIP courses for Lopsidedness (see red square at bottom right). The university was much more uneven than TIP, having almost a quarter in the Top-Heavy zone.

Appendix II

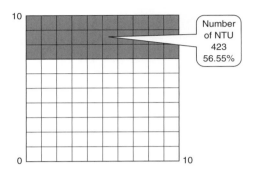

The number of respondents who scored NTU 8, 9 or 10 on the vertical axis (Y = 8, 9 or 10) 11(Questions)×68(persons)=748

NTU	8	9	10	Total	%
Q1	17	10	2	29	42.65%
Q2	23	15	2	40	58.82%
Q3	10	14	5	29	42.65%
Q4	14	17	5	36	52.94%
Q5	19	18	6	43	63.24%
Q6	16	14	5	35	51.47%
Q7	21	13	6	40	58.82%
Q8	17	14	2	33	48.53%
Q9	27	13	2	42	61.76%
Q10	20	18	10	48	70.59%
Q11	18	26	4	48	70.59%
Total	202	172	49	423	56.55%

*It is abundantly clear that the university **does** succeed in its mission. 56.55% of respondents rate their courses 8 out of 10 or better on the values which the university proclaims. The question is rather what the university neglects in its drive for linearly measured merit. When students absorb information from above but do not genuinely think for themselves, when they are deadly serious but rarely playful, when they compete with one another but do hot help and sustain one another, and when they achieve merit which they have not them-selves defined, then is something missing?*

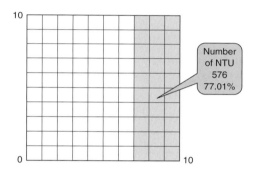

Number of NTU
576
77.01%

The number of respondents who scored TIP 8, 9 or 10 on the horizontal axis (X=8, 9 or 10) 11(Questions)×68(persons)=748

TIP	8	9	10	Total	%
Q1	20	26	2	48	70.59%
Q2	34	18	2	54	79.41%
Q3	21	22	7	50	73.53%
Q4	24	22	6	52	76.47%
Q5	20	29	6	55	80.88%
Q6	27	18	5	50	73.53%
Q7	19	28	2	49	72.06%
Q8	29	22	2	53	77.94%

TIP	8	9	10	Total	%
Q9	24	26	3	53	77.94%
Q10	21	28	9	58	85.29%
Q11	29	22	3	54	79.41%
Total	**268**	**261**	**47**	**576**	**77.01%**

The results above show that TIP is strong precisely where the university's courses are weakest. Students are immersed in intense and unforgettable experiences. They think for themselves. They discover the sense of play vital to innovation. They sustain and support each other's efforts to create in a family atmosphere. Despite the imposing edifice of science they find the strength and confidence to ring changes. Moreover the strength of TIP students on the horizontal measure outscores the university on the vertical dimension. 77.01%, nearly three-quarters, score TIP from 8 to 10. TIP also runs the university extremely close on the vertical dimensions, sometimes exceeding it.

Appendix III

The number of respondents who scored of NTU and TIP in the top right reconciliation zone in the Grid (X≥8∩Y≥8) 11(Questions)×68 (persons) = 748

Top-Right	NTU	%	TIP	%
Q1	3	4.41%	30	44.12%
Q2	2	2.94%	22	32.35%
Q3	2	2.94%	30	44.12%
Q4	0	0.00%	34	50.00%
Q5	5	7.35%	32	47.06%
Q6	6	8.82%	33	48.53%
Q7	8	11.76%	24	35.29%
Q8	3	4.41%	27	39.71%
Q9	6	8.82%	29	42.65%
Q10	5	7.35%	30	44.12%
Q11	3	4.41%	23	33.82%
Total	**43**	**5.75%**	**314**	**41.98%**

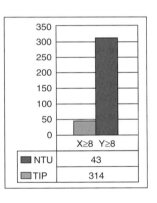

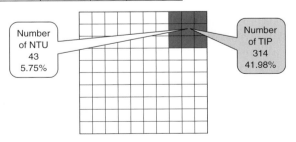

The aim of the TIP programme is to teach students to innovate by combining contrasting values at a high level of intensity. It seeks not lateral or vertical thinking but both, not playfulness or seriousness, but the first in the service of the second, not just the merit authorities want but the merit which students have defined, not just fair competition but competing at cooperating. It is therefore extremely significant that 41.98% scored TIP in the Reconciliation Zone at top right of the Grid, indicating that they rated the programme from 8 to 10 on both dimensions. Only 5.75% placed university courses in that zone, perhaps because this was not their aim. Should the university's mission be reconceived?

Appendix IV

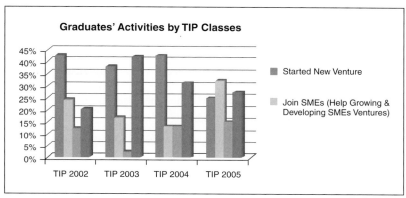

Graduates' Activities by TIP Classes

- Started New Venture
- Join SMEs (Help Growing & Developing SMEs Ventures)

TIP 2002 TIP 2003 TIP 2004 TIP 2005

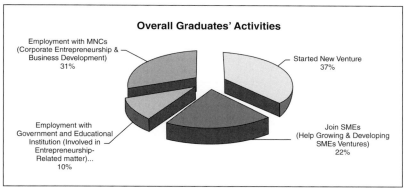

Overall Graduates' Activities

- Employment with MNCs (Corporate Entrepreneurship & Business Development) 31%
- Employment with Government and Educational Institution (Involved in Entrepreneurship-Related matter)... 10%
- Started New Venture 37%
- Join SMEs (Help Growing & Developing SMEs Ventures) 22%

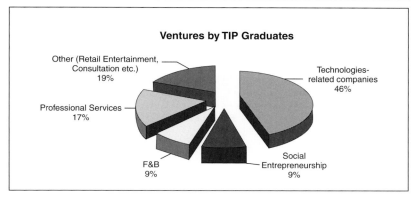

Ventures by TIP Graduates

- Other (Retail Entertainment, Consultation etc.) 19%
- Professional Services 17%
- F&B 9%
- Technologies-related companies 46%
- Social Entrepreneurship 9%

Appendix V

Business Ventures OT Start-ups by TIP Granduates

S/No	Name	TIP	Company Name	Industry
1	Chia Yeow Kheng Roderick	1	Spiral Communications Pte Ltd	Design & Printing
2	Chia Hsiang Yang / Kenneth Yap	1	Tiong Bahru Porridge	F&B (Venture has been sold)
3	Elite Wee	1	Mindsharpener (S) Pte Ltd	Education
4	Kong Fern Chiang	1	Fresh@Work Printing Service	Service
5	Kong Fern Chiang	1	4Media Pte Ltd	Design Printing
6	Lee Kah Howe	1	ST Consultancy Pte Ltd	IT
7	Lee Kah Mun Vincent	1	Inflexion Corporation Pte Ltd	Biotech
8	Somasundaram Krishna	1	Aujix Microsystems Singapore	Business Consultant
9	Tan-Chen Geng Xin Gena	1	GX Enterprise	Entertainment
10	Teo Siew Hin Ruby	1	Stalford Holdings Pte Ltd	Education
11	Ong Chin Kai	1	SMS2All Pte Ltd	Mobile Technology
12	Wong Sin Hin Frederick	1	Moodoo Design	Product Design
13	Ng Sze Siong Daniel	1	FulArc Pte Ltd	Marketing
14	Darren Loi	1	AcuLearn Pte Ltd	IT
15	Peng Chun Hsien	1	Avocada Pte Ltd	IT

S/No	Name	TIP	Company Name	Industry
16	Chiam Siang Roung Kenneth	2	AMCIS HomeStay	Service
17	Goh Yi Peng Jann, Ho Hwee Shi Jan	2	AppleStiz	F&B
18	Tan Soon Meng	2	Explore Marine Pte Ltd	Education
19	Tang Shiuh Huei	2	S H Tang & Associates	Accountancy
20	Vincent Ang / Sim Chin Soong	2	Swisston Pte Ltd	IT, Design
21	Wee Kien Meng	2	MagicianS Network (Singapore)	Entertainment
22	Yeo Choon Hin Melvin and Saw Lin Kiat	2	Trust Motto Pte Ltd, Organic Food Biz	F&B
23	Yeo Choon Hin Melvin and Saw Lin Kiat	2	HealthyLife Pte Ltd	F&B
24	Low Kwek Ping, Kezene	2	Happe Holdings Pte Ltd	Entertainment
25	Jann Goh	2	Geowalker Pte Ltd	IT
26	Ken Poh, May Soon, Justin Loc	3	PD Scientific Pte Ltd	IT, Retail
27	Manfred Seow Khim Kiong	3	GistLabs	Biotech
28	Meliza Bte Mohd Salim	3	Romance d'Amour	Retail
29	Willson Tang	3	Mind's Eye Media	Design & Service
30	Derrick Sim	3	NanoFrontier Pte Ltd	Nanotech
31	Derrick Sim	3	PD Design Studio Pte Ltd	Design & Animation
32	Ngaim Tee W'oh	3	Nvovio and Renewe	Retail

S/No	Name	TIP	Company Name	Industry
33	Ngaim Tee W'oh	3	Renewe	Product Design
34	Chye Choon Hoong, Adrian and Arif Nugroho	3	MediaFreaks	Media & Animation
35	Chye Choon Hoong, Adrian and Arif Nugroho	3	Learning Horizon	Education
36	Lu Yong An, Andy	2	NLone Pte Ltd	Service
37	Beh Wah Yan	4	Creston Pte Ltd	IT
38	Harry Foo	4	EVO Entertainment	Entertainment
39	Ezen HO	4	Grand Sun	Spa & Beauty
40	Vincent Lim	4	Buddy Pte Ltd	Retail
41	Mohd Adil	4	Softphone Evangelist	VoIP Technology
42	Nelson Ong	4	CT Graphic	Design & Printing
43	Tommy Ong	4		Biotech
44	Tan Kar Wee	4	Lam Chuan Pte Ltd	Retail & Construction
45	Ng Kok Siang	5	UFO Laboratory Glass Services	Service
46	Mahesh	5	Human Touch	Business Consultant

Appendix VI

The overall effect of the different programme of choices, NTU vs. TIP

	MEAN		R-SQUARES	P-VALUE
	NTU	TIP		
Question 1	33.26	57.38	0.342397	P<0.01
Question 2	33.66	53.52	0.253615	P<0.01
Question 3	28.60	56.37	0.362361	P<0.01
Question 4	31.54	59.78	0.345391	P<0.01
Question 5	34.80	49.45	0.247668	P<0.01
Question 6	33.60	57.62	0.251277	P<0.01
Question 7	41.78	56.06	0.072604	P<0.01
Question 8	34.24	52.91	0.245644	P<0.01
Question 9	33.94	53.63	0.266653	P<0.01
Question 10	35.51	55.59	0.220322	P<0.01
Question 11	34.34	56.86	0.137630	P<0.01
Total effect	**375.27**	**609.17**	**0.411390**	**P<0.01**

Here we regress the dependent variable to find out the overall effectiveness of the programme of choices (multiplying the values from the X axis and the Y axis). The independent variable X is a dummy variable which equals 1 when a respondent refers to the TIP education programme and equals 0 when a respondent refers to the NTU educational programme.

From the regression, we find that the average score for NTU is 375.2941 and that the TIP score is some 241.2941 higher than NTU.

This means that the TIP programme delivers 64% more of the values measured here than does the average of NTU programmes.

The R-squared is 0.411390, which means that 41% of the difference in the scores comes from the different forms of education offered by NTU and TIP programmes. The t-statistic is 9.677546 and is highly significant statistically at the <0.01 level.

Appendix VII

**The impact of the programme on the vertical axis
(Traditional Objectives)
NTU vs. TIP**

	MEAN		R-SQUARES	P-VALUE
	NTU	TIP		
Question 1a	7.06	7.02	0.002017	P>0.05
Question 2a	7.24	6.74	0.017636	P>0.05
Question 3a	6.85	7.19	0.006742	P>0.05
Question 4a	7.54	7.50	0.000151	P>0.05
Question 5a	7.76	6.81	0.038278	P<0.05
Question 6a	7.82	7.07	0.001477	P>0.05
Question 7a	7.22	7.06	0.011647	P>0.05
Question 8a	7.29	6.88	0.004204	P>0.05
Question 9a	7.07	6.84	0.000207	P>0.05
Question 10a	7.00	6.94	0.047226	P<0.01
Question 11a	7.75	6.26	0.113135	P<0.01
Total effect	**80.60**	**76.31**	**0.024594**	**P>0.05**

Appendix VIII

The impact of the programme on the horizontal axis (Non-Traditional Objectives) NTU vs. TIP

	MEAN		R-SQUARES	P-VALUE
	NTU	**TIP**		
Question 1b	4.78	7.97	0.499134	$P < 0.01$
Question 2b	4.66	7.94	0.470816	$P < 0.01$
Question 3b	4.22	7.84	0.438878	$P < 0.01$
Question 4b	4.24	7.97	0.522575	$P < 0.01$
Question 5b	4.69	8.35	0.500844	$P < 0.01$
Question 6b	4.53	8.15	0.47165	$P < 0.01$
Question 7b	4.65	7.94	0.180605	$P < 0.01$
Question 8b	5.75	7.69	0.418081	$P < 0.01$
Question 9b	4.85	7.84	0.463779	$P < 0.01$
Question 10b	4.76	8.01	0.501014	$P < 0.01$
Question 11b	4.57	7.90	0.461108	$P < 0.01$
Total effect	**51.70**	**87.60**	**0.612989**	**$P < 0.01$**

General index

Index of dilemmas
and reconciliations